The Science of Esports

T0384841

The Science of Esports draws from contemporary research and coach expertise to examine esports athlete health and performance from a range of disciplinary perspectives, including physiology, psychology, sociology, and nutrition. The rapid expansion of the esports industry has elevated competitive video gaming into the realm of high performance, requiring players, coaches, and practitioners to implement interdisciplinary approaches to performance support.

This book covers key topic areas such as:

- What esports is and its similarities and differences to sport
- Game-specific training
- Physiological and psychological consideration for esports athletes
- Social aspects of player performance and the social environment of esports
- Esports coaching and structure of esports performance environments
- Technology and its use in esports
- Safeguarding, cheating, and gambling

This book includes worked examples and case studies to allow immediate implementation into practice for esports athletes and coaches. It summarises the current state of research to inform researchers and identify gaps in knowledge. This book is critical reading for students of esports and related courses. It serves as the first scientific resource designed to provide athletes, coaches, and practitioners with interdisciplinary insights into esports health and performance.

Craig McNulty, PhD, is a lecturer and researcher at Queensland University of Technology, Australia. His research areas include athlete and e'athlete exercise physiology, oxygen uptake kinetics, and physiological measures in esports. He supervises several doctoral students across topics, including energy expenditure in esports, women's esports athlete health and performance, and sleep and sleep-behaviours in esports. Craig was a founding board member of the Esports Research Network, which was founded in 2019.

Remco Polman, PhD, is the executive dean of the Institute of Health and Wellbeing at Federation University, Australia. Although a sport and exercise psychologist by training, his research is multi- and inter-disciplinary in nature. He is particularly interested in the psychological determinants of performance and well-being in athletes with particular expertise in stress, coping, and emotions. Remco is a chartered psychologist by the British Psychological Society and an accredited sport and exercise psychologist with the Health Care and Professions Council in the United Kingdom.

Matthew Watson is the director of Learning & Development at the International Federation of Esports Coaches (IFoEC). Matt is responsible for designing and delivering esports coaching and performance programmes in a range of academic and applied settings. Matt has published a number of peer-reviewed scientific articles as part of his ongoing PhD in coaching at the German Sport University in Cologne, and lectures in esports at the University of Northampton.

Kabir Bubna is a research assistant with The International Federation of Esports Coaches. Kabir has achieved a BSc (Hons) and Masters by Research in Sports, Coaching, and Physical Education. His masters' thesis focused on understanding coaches' perceptions of the development of collective behaviour. With his educational background, Kabir has also developed a critical understanding of talent identification and development, skill acquisition, and effective coaching practice in traditional sporting contexts. Since then, he has taken his knowledge and applied it towards esports academia and coaching practice in this novel industry.

The Science of Esports

Craig McNulty, Remco Polman,
Matthew Watson, and Kabir Bubna

NEW YORK AND LONDON

Designed cover image: Getty

First published 2024
by Routledge
605 Third Avenue, New York, NY 10158

and by Routledge
4 Park Square, Milton Park, Abingdon, Oxon, OX14 4RN

Routledge is an imprint of the Taylor & Francis Group, an Informa business

© 2024 Craig McNulty, Remco Polman, Matthew Watson, and Kabir Bubna

The right of Craig McNulty, Remco Polman, Matthew Watson, and
Kabir Bubna to be identified as authors of this work has been asserted in
accordance with sections 77 and 78 of the Copyright, Designs and Patents
Act 1988.

ISBN: 978-1-032-34571-0 (hbk)
ISBN: 978-1-032-34485-0 (pbk)
ISBN: 978-1-003-32238-2 (ebk)

DOI: 10.4324/9781003322382

Typeset in Times New Roman
by codeMantra

Contents

Figures, tables, and boxes

Figures

Tables

Boxes

Acknowledgements

The authors wish to thank the following experts for their specialist contributions to the book.

James 'Torok' Thomsen – League of Legends Coach; Board of Experts (International Federation of Esports Coaches)

Jack J Williams – Data Scientist and Founder of iTero Gaming

James 'Jimmah' Forshaw – Australian professional Rocket League Coach

Callum Abbott – Sport & Exercise Psychologist for Team Endpoint, Head of Performance for Akolyte Esports

1   What is esports?

Craig McNulty

1.1   Introduction

Esports, also known as electronic sports, is a form of competitive video gaming that has rapidly gained popularity in recent years. It involves organised competitions between individuals or teams who play video games, typically first-person shooter or multiplayer online battle arena games, often in front of a live audience and/or online spectators. Esports tournaments are held globally and are often broadcasted through online streaming platforms, such as Twitch or YouTube, attracting millions of viewers.

Esports has grown into a massive industry, with players competing for large cash prizes and sponsorship deals. Professional esports players are now considered athletes, and their skills and strategies are as highly respected and admired as those of traditional sport athletes. In addition to professional gaming competitions, esports has been embraced by many schools and universities as a legitimate form of athletic competition, with secondary school and university teams being established to compete against other schools. In addition, scholarships are provided by educational institutions to attract the best e'athletes. The growth of esports has been fuelled by advancements in technology, particularly the widespread availability of high-speed internet and powerful gaming computers. This has made it possible for players to compete in online tournaments and for fans to watch matches in real-time from anywhere in the world. In recent years, esports has also been recognised by the International Olympic Committee (IOC) as a sport, with discussions about including esports in the Olympic games and the inaugural IOC Olympic Esports week organised in June 2023 in collaboration with the Singapore National Olympic Committee.

Esports encompasses more than just the competitive aspect of video gaming. It also includes the economic, business, performance, and social structures that form the foundation of this global phenomenon. This chapter aims to introduce the reader to esports in its collective form, from its early history in computing labs and arcades to its modern spectator-packed arena competitions. To set the stage, this chapter outlines existing definitions of esports, summarises the broad scope of esports business (from computer hardware to competition organisers), and finally examines the global economics of esports currently, and its expectations for the future.

DOI: 10.4324/9781003322382-1

1.2   Recent history

As with any evolving global structure, there is disagreement on the moment in time at which esports or competitive gaming was first introduced. It may have been as early as 1958, with the invention of what is widely considered the first video game, Tennis for Two: a two-player game developed using a DuMont Lab Oscilloscope at the Brookhaven National Laboratory in New York, United States. Or perhaps it was in 1972 when the video game *Spacewar!* (1962) was played in a competitive tournament format, with the overall winner being awarded a 12-month subscription to *Rolling Stone* magazine. It's challenging to pinpoint the moment that competitive video gaming entered the scene. Despite this, the 1980 Atari Space Invaders Championship is widely considered to be the first large-scale esports competition. The event, sponsored by Atari Inc., saw 10,000 players compete in the tournament to promote the new release of Space Invaders on the Atari 2,600 console, with an arcade machine being awarded for the first place. The following four decades have seen esports exponentially grow in competitive players, prize pool value, global competitions, and spectators. Figure 1.1 provides a timeline summary of some of the major defining moments of growth and innovation in esports from the 1980s to 2020s.

The late 1990s and 2000s marked a significant period in which esports established itself as a legitimate professional career, forming numerous professional organisations and leagues, such as AMD Professional Gamers League and Cyberathlete Professional League (founded in 1997), and later, Major League Gaming and Electronic Sports League (later retitled ESL). These leagues, not dissimilar to the many global and national sporting leagues, organise and host competitions for either single game or multiple game titles. Leagues improved player access to amateur and professional career pathways, and through partnerships with online and televised broadcasting, they exposed the world to an organised and competitive seasonal structure in video gaming not seen before. As of 2022, there are close to 100 active tier 1 esports leagues globally. As esports has grown, so has its acceptance as a legitimate professional career option. Professional esports players became recognised as professional athletes as early as 2001 in Russia (esports was later removed from the Russian Government's list of sports in 2006, only to be reinstated as a sport in 2017), and in 2003 in China. Since then, many countries with even a modest esports player base have since recognised esports as either a sport or a legitimate professional career. Some examples of this include:

- In the United States, the definition of "sport" varies between organisations, with some recognising esports as a sport while others do not.
- South Korea is one of the largest esports markets in the world, and the government has recognised esports as a sport and provided support for the industry.
- The Chinese government recognises esports as a sport and has supported its development, with plans to build more esports venues and establish a national esports industry park.

- In France, esports is recognised as a sport and is governed by the French Esports Federation.
- The United Kingdom government has not officially recognised esports as a sport.

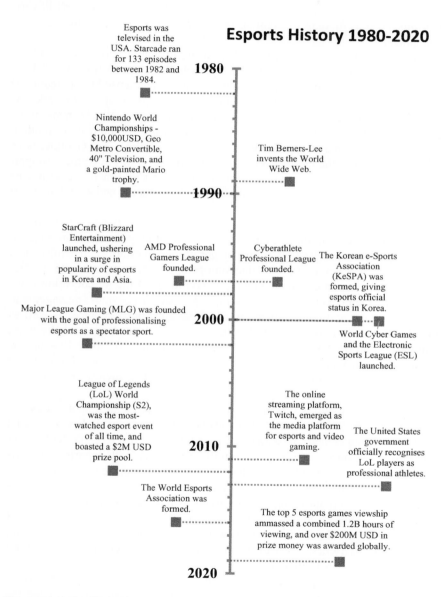

Figure 1.1 A timeline of key events in the history of esports from 1980 to 2020.

It is worth noting that the recognition of esports as a sport can impact various aspects such as funding, taxation, and the regulations surrounding the industry. It is difficult to determine which national governments specifically fund esports, as the level of investment and support can vary greatly among countries. However, there have been instances where governments have shown support for esports in various forms, such as funding for training facilities, tournaments, and infrastructure development.

In South Korea, the government has been a strong supporter of esports and has invested in the development of the industry, including the construction of dedicated esports stadiums. In China, the government has recognised the potential of esports as a source of economic growth and has taken steps to support the industry, including investment in gaming companies and infrastructure development. In the United States, the government has been more cautious in its approach to funding esports, although some state governments, such as California and Georgia, have made investments in the industry. Overall, while the level of government support for esports can vary greatly among countries, it is clear that many governments consider the potential for esports to contribute to the economy and are taking steps to support its growth.

Over the last few years, we have seen the rising popularity and growth of the esports industry develop into a multi-tiered system of players and team progression. Competitions and leagues are no longer unique to established professional players. As well, from an esports education perspective, as of 2021, 95 distinctive tertiary degrees in esports are being delivered by 74 higher education institutes globally (Jenny et al., 2021), covering topics such as business management, media production and communication, coaching and sports science, as well as game design. Many universities and tertiary institutes boast competitive esports teams, with their own practice arenas, and management staff, not unlike university/varsity sport. More recently, high school and secondary education institutes have followed a similar example to universities, with their own teams and practice areas.

Esports spectatorship is now on par with some of the biggest sporting events on the planet. The 2021 League of Legends World Championship final boasted a total of 74 million concurrent viewers. To put this in perspective, the NFL Super Bowl during the same year drew in 96 million viewers. With esports being primarily viewed via online platforms that are free to use and accessible to anyone with a stable internet connection, the limitations normally imposed on viewership by television broadcasting (due to broadcasting rights, regional popularity, and censorship) are no longer a barrier to global access. In the first quarter of 2022, 8.06 billion hours of live streams were viewed across the online streaming platforms such as Twitch, YouTube Gaming, and Facebook Gaming (7.13 billion hours were viewed on Twitch alone).

With the birth of esports occurring only in the last half-century, its evolution from modest competitions and prize pools, which often only attracted the truly die-hard players and fans, to today's global enterprise is nothing short of astounding. With the continued growth in viewership, broadcasting, economic and business development, and academic-lead research, esports has already established itself as one of the premier entertainment industries in the world, with no sign of slowing.

1.3 Definitions

Before we continue further, it is important that we define the term 'esports'. Naturally, anyone with involvement in this industry likely has a definition of esports in mind, and depending on their discipline and background that definition may vary from the perspective of a performance and training coach, to a sports scientist, or to a psychologist. With increasingly broad practitioner and academic interest developing in esports over the last two decades, specifying a general definition of esports is important. An early scientific definition by Wagner (2006), adapted from a definition of sport proposed by Tiedemann (2004), stated that:

> *eSports* is an area of sport activities in which people develop and train mental or physical abilities in the use of information and communication technologies.

More recently, Jenny and colleagues (2017) disputed Wagner's definition due to its ambiguity (despite Wagner's attempts to draw a more specific definition of esports from Tiedemann's definition of sport). Jenny and colleagues (2017) argued the need to distinguish esports from recreational gaming by including aspects of organised competition to the evolving definition of esports, as well as the online streaming nature of esports. Further to this, Pedraza-Ramirez and colleagues (2020) developed a comprehensive definition of esports, based on prior sporting definitions but without the necessity of physical activity (despite a number of activities which require minimal physicality, such as chess and bridge being recognised by the International Olympic Committee as sports):

> Esports is the casual or organized competitive activity of playing specific video games that provide professional and/or personal development to the player. This practice is facilitated by electronic systems, either computers, consoles, tablets, or mobile phones, on which teams and individual players practice and compete online and/or in local-area-network tournaments at the professional or amateur level. The games are established by ranking systems and competitions and are regulated by official leagues. This structure provides players a sense of being part of a community and facilitates mastering expertise in fine-motor coordination and perceptual-cognitive skills, particularly but not exclusively, at higher levels of performance.

Recently, Formosa and colleagues (2022) conducted a systematic review of 461 peer-reviewed papers which included some form of definition of esports. The authors noted that from 1990 onwards, there are more citations of individual definitions than to and singular and commonly cited definition. As was the case with 'sport' for many years (and arguably, is still ongoing), the definition of esports will likely continue to shift until there is some semblance of academic and practitioner consensus globally. For the remainder of this book, the authors will be using the Pedraza-Ramirez and colleagues' (2020) definition of esports. Adopting this definition also implies that those individuals playing esports should be considered athletes. As such, we will refer to esports players as e'athletes.

1.4   Esports as a sport

To begin understanding regional and global structures of esports, we must have a general understanding of these constructs within sport. With sport arguably being documented in human history from as early as 70,000 BCE (Crowther, 2007), it has had quite a period of time to develop into the global enterprise as we know it today. From competitive activities such as spear-throwing, sprinting, and wrestling recorded in cave painting art from an early era in human recorded history, to the first recorded Olympic Games in 776 BCE, and through to modern-day sporting structures, sport is heavily intwined with human history. With such a lasting presence, spanning numerous eras of human civilisation, it is no surprise that sport in its existing structures has acted as the framework for the development of esports from its early history to the global sensation it is today.

With its development spanning thousands of years, and its globalisation over the past couple of centuries, sport has implemented itself in many facets of society, politics, and industry. Esports to many degrees has incorporated modern constructs of sport to its own development and organisational structure. Whether esports is considered a sport by definition is regionally exclusive, and specific to government organisations where esports competition takes place. Despite the inclusion or exclusion (at least, currently) of esports within the broader sport governance of nations and national unions, esports is undeniably analogous with sport. Grassroots esports, formed from local clubs within and external to secondary schools and universities, are akin to many sports development structures, globally. The parallels of sport and esports span player/team rankings, distinct disciplines, and training structures.

E'athlete rankings are primarily defined by the Elo statistical model (Elo, 1978) built into algorithms within the many ranking systems across esports titles. This model is based on pairwise comparisons of normally distributed scores to determine the win probability (Bisberg & Cardona-Rivera, 2019). Performance in a ranked esports match, guided by a win or a loss, will see an athlete increase or decrease in rank, respectively. However, the numerical difference in the change of a rank following a win or a loss is entirely dependent on the current probability (based on the existing rank) that a player will win or lose a match. For example, two identically ranked players would increase or decrease by an equal amount following a win or a loss. However, in an example where a highly ranked player competed against a much lower-ranked player, we would see variation in the rank movement following a win or a loss. If the lower-ranked player, against likely odds, defeated the higher-ranked player, they would increase in rank by a value greater than that if it were an equally-ranked match. Similarly, a win for the higher-ranked competitor would only see a fractional increase in rank in comparison to an equally-ranked match. This ranking system is comparative to those used within sport, and particularly individual sports. It may assist with appropriate matchmaking as well as inform team selection and player recruitment.

As with sport, there are similarities yet distinct differences in the physiological and cognitive demands of esports across varying titles. Although both tennis players and football players require high cardiovascular fitness, muscular power, and strategical thinking to perform well, there are individual needs that differ between the sports. From a cardiovascular fitness perspective, tennis players rely on higher intensity and shorter bouts of activity, whereas football players must maintain constant movement across a match, with intervals of high-intensity (sprint) fitness. Also, where hand-eye coordination dominates tennis, outfield footballers require increased foot-eye coordination. Esports, like sport, is a hypernym that encompasses many titles (more broadly, genres) of esports competition and play. Each esports title comprises its own discrete style of gameplay, objectives, and rules, which require distinct physiological and cognitive capabilities to perform at the elite level. Where League of Legends (LoL) requires a higher focus on strategy and team and opposition map awareness, Counter Strike: Global Offensive (CS:GO) demands a greater emphasis on reaction and response time, and speed and accuracy. Chapter 3 discusses physiological and cognitive needs of players in relation to esports titles in further depth.

Training structures in sport vary from social, amateur, and elite/professional. While social or amateur sportspeople or teams may often practise once or twice per week (through school or a community club), and compete weekly, elite and professional athletes will likely train and compete in a full-time capacity. During pre-season and in-season, full-time athletes will probably train most days of the week, with perhaps one or two 'rest/recovery' days depending on the competition calendar. Training may differ to address muscular fitness, cardiovascular fitness, and critical skill development. Esports training has been criticised due to its heavy focus on dedicating many hours of gameplay as its primary modality of training. Abbott and Colleagues (2023) concluded that the professional training structure, or 'grind-culture' within LoL is highly inducive to player burnout. This is a sentiment generally shared across many esports titles. Although, esports training and coaching culture has seen somewhat of a paradigm shift in recent years, with a modern focus that aims to reduce athlete fatigue and burnout. Apart from grinding, esports training may also occur within isolated environments, relying on software such as AimLab (aimlab.gg) to improve discrete skills. Scrimmages, or 'scrims', is another common approach to esports practice. Scrims involve two teams competing against each other outside of an official competition or league. Scrims are not dissimilar to a 'friendly' or 'exhibition' match seen in many sporting codes. Scrims allow teams to test new tactics that may be seen as too risky within a competitive league or a tournament.

1.5   The esports business

Esports titles are commonly free-to-play, with some of the most popular titles (such as Defence of the Ancients 2 (DOTA 2) and LoL) requiring relatively low computer specifications and performance to run. As well, anyone with an internet connection and capable device are able to spectate every esports and video gaming – from the League of Legends World Championships to a near-endless array of content streamers – without additional costs or subscriptions required for other movie, television, or sport streaming services. This ease of access has been attributed to esports' massive growth and popularity, with Newzoo (2022) reporting hundreds of millions of new players and spectators joining the esports ranks (so to speak) each year. In fact, esports spectators were estimated at 532 million in 2022, with a predicted increase to 640 million by 2025 (Newzoo, 2022).

Both amateur and semi-professional esports also contribute to the overall growth of the industry. E'athlete opportunities and development within secondary schools, as well as colleges and universities globally, are expanding. Like many other sporting programs, universities, and colleges (and occasionally, secondary, and even primary schools) around the world have developed esports programs, with coaching staff, competitions, and financial support available. Additionally, Jenny and colleagues (2021) identified approximately 75 different higher education institutions worldwide which offer degrees or certifications in esports. Indicating that not only practice, but also research and academia in esports is growing. This list is being continually updated as more institutes incorporate esports into their curricula.

The esports industry, while its foundations are its athletes and spectators, is tethered by an interconnected ecosystem consisting of broadcasting platforms, game publishers, organisers, teams, and sponsors. Meanwhile, video game and esports titles themselves are similarly bound by an interrelated web of software and hardware developers, game publishers, game developers, streaming services, and distributors. The esports ecosystem also illustrates the global economics of esports, which has seen exponential growth over the years.

1.6   Global economics

Esports continually increases in growth in terms of player-base, organisations, broadcasting, spectatorship, and social acceptance as a legitimate enterprise. This exponential growth is also characterised by the global economic impact of esports over the last few decades. It's not simply the evolution from relatively small cash prizes for local and regional tournaments to the $40M USD prize pool of the 2021 *Defence of the Ancients 2* World Championship that has impacted the global esports economy. In 2019, the entire esports industry revenue was valued at $25B USD (Ahn et al., 2020) across multiple sectors including professional players and teams, video game publishers, broadcasting platforms, related products, leagues and tournaments, and digital tools (Figure 1.2).

For comparison, the combined European Football market recorded €25.2B ($26.55B USD) in revenue in 2019. In *The Book of Esports* (2020), Collis proposed an Entire Esports Ecosystem (EEE), which was used as the basis for the 2019 industry valuation of $25B USD. EEE depicts six categories which impact the esports economy. The categories, and some examples, are outlined in the Table 1.1.

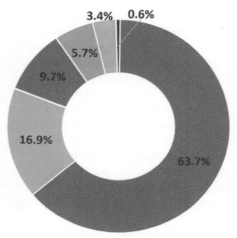

- Game Publishers (GPs): $15.85B (63.7%)
- Streaming Platforms (SPs): $2.41B (9.7%)
- Digital Tools (DTs): $0.84B (3.4%)
- Teams, Professionals, and Streamers (TPSs): $4.20B (16.9%)
- Physical Products (PPs): $1.42B (5.7%)
- Leagues and Tournaments (LTs): $0.14B (0.6%)

Figure 1.2 Total esports market revenue size estimate per sector in 2019 (Ahn et al., 2020).

Table 1.1 The Entire Esports Ecosystem

Esports Sector	Sector Description	Examples
Publishers and games	Companies which develop, produce, and sell esports titles	Riot Games®, Valve®, Epic Games®
Leagues and tournaments	Organisations which host and promote competitions	CS:GO Pro League, ESL Pro League, League of Legends World Championship Series
Streaming and media platforms	Platforms for viewing esports competitions, or professional video game streamers	Twitch, YouTube, Facebook Live
Teams and professionals	The players which compete in competitions	Lee 'Faker' Sang-hyeok (LoL), Johan 'n0tail' Sundstein (DOTA2), Richard 'Ninja' Tyler Blevins (Streamer).
Digital gaming products	Software tools which facilitate esports	Aimlab, Discord, GameSpot
Physical gaming products	Hardware components and lifestyle products	Corsair®, Secret Lab®, Logitech®

Adapted from Collis (2020).

As outlined in Figure 1.1, video game publishers such as Activision-Blizzard and Riot account for ~64% of esports industry revenue in 2019. As video games are the foundation of esports, this shouldn't be too surprising. What is interesting, however, is the way in which many of these games collect revenue. Unlike a typical single player, or a story-based game, which requires an outright purchase for either a physical or a digital copy of the game, many of the major esports titles are considered free-to-play (FTP) games. This means that downloading and playing the unabridged title is completely free (apart from the requirement of a stable internet connection). So then how are the video game publishers achieving such high revenues for their games? Games such as Fortnite, LoL, DOTA 2, and Player Unknown Battleground use a microtransaction model to drive their revenue. The initial argument for this approach (and a clearly successful one) was the need to have a large player-base, which could be more easily achieved by offering an FTP game, as opposed to a high initial purchase cost (which might dissuade video game enthusiasts from purchasing the title). Although the use of microtransactions, such as in-game loot boxes, has come under scrutiny for their similarities to gambling, or their potential to create a 'pay-to-win' scenario, the revenue model has supported far broader access to esports titles than its pay-to-play counterparts.

The income of professional players, teams, and streamer made up 17% ($4.2B USD) of the global revenue in esports in 2019. This valuation included prize-pool winnings, sponsorships, and exclusivity deals. Although professional video game streamers may earn an income from competitive matches and tournaments, their primary revenue is based on their streaming channel's viewership in the form of a subscriptions and one-off monetary 'gifts'. In addition to the revenue of an individual player, the top esports teams have recorded earnings in the tens of millions of USD. Team Liquid (primarily DOTA 2 and CS:GO), OG (DOTA 2), and Evil Geniuses (DOTA 2) have reported combined winnings of over $100M USD. In *This is Esports (And How to Spell It)*, Paul Chaloner raises concerns about the current 'over-valuation' of some of the top professional esports teams. As of May 2022, Team Liquid's valuation was estimated at $415M USD, despite a total revenue of less than 10% of that value. Perhaps this valuation provides some insights into the future expectations of success of professional esports teams, and by extension, the esports industry itself.

Streaming platforms were identified as the second-highest revenue source in 2019, contributing 9.7% ($2.4B USD) to the total esports revenue. Since its inception in 2011, following the success of its predecessor *Justin.tv*, Twitch has been the foundation for video game broadcasting in the form of live streams. Several other streaming platforms have since surfaced, with other popular platforms including YouTube Gaming and Facebook Gaming. Twitch reported $2.6B USD in revenue in 2021, the majority of which was earned through advertising. Exclusivity deals between streaming platforms and some of the most viewed streamers is not uncommon.

1.7 Summary

Esports is a rapidly growing industry involving competitive video gaming between individuals or teams in front of live or online audiences. It has become a legitimate form of athletic competition, with e'athletes competing for cash prizes and sponsorships. Esports has gained recognition globally as a legitimate professional career option, with close to 100 active tier 1 esports leagues worldwide. The recognition of esports as a sport varies between countries, but many see the potential for esports to contribute to the economy and are taking steps to support its growth.

Most esports titles are free-to-play and accessible to anyone with an internet connection and capable device. This ease of access has contributed to the industry's massive growth, with hundreds of millions of new players and spectators joining each year. Esports programs are also expanding in secondary schools and colleges globally, with some offering degrees or certifications in esports. The industry is tethered by an interconnected ecosystem consisting of broadcasting platforms, game publishers, organisers, teams, and sponsors, illustrating the global economics of esports.

The global economic impact of esports was $25B USD in 2019, with video game publishers accounting for approximately 64% of industry revenue. Microtransactions drive their revenue, and professional players, teams, and streamer income make up 17%. Streaming platforms contribute 9.7% to the revenue. The top esports teams have reported combined winnings of over $100M USD, with concerns raised about their over-valuation. Twitch is the foundation for video game broadcasting, with advertising being its major source of revenue.

References

Abbott, C., Watson, M., and Birch, P. (2023). Perceptions of effective training practices in League of Legends: A qualitative exploration. *Journal of Electronic Gaming and Esports, 1*, 1–11.

Ahn, J., Collis, W., and Jenny, S. (2020). The one billion dollar myth: Methods for sizing the massively undervalued esports revenue landscape. *International Journal of Esports, 1*(1). https://www.ijesports.org/article/15/html

Aimlab. (2022). Aimlab. https://aimlab.gg/

Bisberg, A. J., and Cardona-Rivera, R. E. (2019). Scope: Selective cross-validation over parameters for Elo. *Fifteenth AAAI Conference on Artificial Intelligence and Interactive Digital Entertainment, 15*(1), 116–122.

Collis, W. (2020). *The Book of Esports*. RosettaBooks.

Crowther, N. B. (2007). *Sport in Ancient Times*. Praeger Publishers.

Elo, A. E. (1978). *The Rating of Chess Players*. The American Chess Foundation.

Formosa, J., O'Donnell, N., Horton, E. M., Türkay, S., Mandryk, R. L., Hawks, M., and Johnson, D. (2022). Definitions of esports: A systematic review and thematic analysis. *Proceedings of the ACM on Human-Computer Interaction, 6*(227), 1–45.

Jenny, S. E., Gawrysiak, J., and Besombes, N. (2021). Esports.edu: An inventory and analysis of global higher educations esports academic programming and curricula. *International Journal of Esports, 1*(1), 1–47.

Jenny, S. E., Manning, R. D., Keiper, M. C., and Olrich, T. W. (2017). Virtual(ly) athletes: where esports fit within the definition of "sport". *Quest, 69*(1), 1–18.

Newzoo. (2022). Global games market report 2022. https://newzoo.com/insights/trend-reports/newzoo-global-games-market-report-2022-free-version

Pedraza-Ramirez, I., Musculus, L., Raab, M., and Laborde, S. (2020). Setting the scientific stage for esports psychology: a systematic review. *International Review of Sport and Exercise Psychology, 13*(1), 319–352. DOI: 10.1080/1750984X.2020.1723122

Tiedemann, C. (September, 2004). Sport (and culture of human motion) for historians, an approach to make the central term(s) more precise. http://claustiedemann.de/tiedemann/documents/VortragCrotone2004Englisch.pdf

Wagner, M. (2006). On the scientific relevance of esports. *International Conference on Internet Computing*, Las Vegas, NV, 437–442.

2 Aspects of game-specific training

*Matthew Watson, Remco Polman,
and Kabir Bubna*

2.1 Introduction

As with traditional sport, training and practice are crucial aspects of esports and undoubtedly take up the most time of all of the activities connected with being a professional player. While it's clear that training and practice are important in order to achieve a high-level of performance in esports, there is lack of consensus on how to effectively spend time in esports. Indeed, there have been relatively few academic studies on training and practice in esports and, as a consequence, little is known about how to train and prepare best for specific games. In this chapter, we will draw from a range of sources to describe some of the common training and practice activities associated with major esports and consider the evidence for their effectiveness.

Before examining training practices in esports, it is important to understand what learning is and the factors which influence this process. Learning motor skills consist of encoding and consolidation. Encoding refers to the process of information to be remembered. Only that can be retrieved that has been stored, and how it can be retrieved depends on how it was stored. Practice, or on-line learning, results in performance increases. Consolidation refers to off-line strengthening of the internal representation in memory following practice. It is probably good to keep in mind that a factor which has consistently been associated with motor learning is sleep. For information to be consolidated into memory, sleep is required. Although learning is seen while practising a motor task, during sleep newly forged neural connections are strengthened resulting in enhanced performance off-line (without additional physical practice). Sleep consolidates (stabilises or enhances) information regarding the motor skill in long-term memory. While the decremental effects of sleep deprivation on performance are well understood, it is important to recognise that sleep is also essential to skill learning (e.g., Blischke & Erlacher, 2007).

There are many other factors coaches should consider which influence memory encoding and consolidation. This includes the e'athletes' emotional state, use of substances and medications, mental health, general health, age or maturity, motivation and interest, and meaningfulness of the information. This indicates that ensuring the e'athletes' good physical and mental health is essential for their learning and performance.

DOI: 10.4324/9781003322382-2

Finally, controlled processing of information has significant limitations in terms of capacity. Hence, our short-term memory can only deal with 7 ± 2 items at a time (Miller, 1956). When we practise tasks and skills for some time, they become automated. This process allows us to use more information by employing perceptual grouping or chunking, enabling the grouping of separate stimuli in meaningful wholes. This process is likely to be particularly important in strategic esports. Hence, chunking results in a reduction in the number of individual stimuli one has to pay attention to. Whereas previous stimuli are processed individually in series they can now be seen as one group. This will speed up information processing because more information can be picked-up at a glance. It will also help in a quicker and easier interpretation of patterns of play and emergence of features when stimuli are viewed in isolation. So, development of esports specific information in memory will help in encoding, organisation, and retrieval of information.

2.2   Training in League of Legends (LoL)

In sport, the development of physical fitness and specific technical or tactical skills has been a central feature of training. Regarding technical skills, historically training methods have been based on cognitive psychological principles, and it is assumed that motor learning is achieved by isolating (either partially or in full) that skill or technique and repeating its execution (grooving in). For example, practising a reverse lay-up in basketball without a defender present, with a defender present, off-the-dribble or after a pass. In this situation, feedback from a coach at various points, particularly in the earlier, developmental stages of training, would be quite usual if not welcomed. Motor learning, or the route from being a novice to an expert performer in this view goes through several stages. Fitts and Posner (1967) put forward a classification on how motor behaviour changes as a function of practice. In the early cognitive stage of this model, skill execution is based on explicit information, rules based, and declarative (what) knowledge, whereas execution of the skill tends to be slow, erratic, effortful, and with significant number of errors. During the associative stage of learning, it becomes easier to detect errors in performance and implement appropriate solutions. The athlete will be able to adapt movements to situational demands. Rather than solving problems, athletes will be able to retrieve solutions which will speed up movement execution. Finally, in the autonomous phase, cognitive involvement is gradually eliminated and knowledge about the skill becomes implicit and proceduralised (focussing on the 'how'), whereas execution is automated, smooth, fast, effortless, and with minimal error.

In many major esports games, and LoL in particular, the training and learning of techniques is quite different. For example, beyond an initial tutorial, most players develop their technical skill while playing the game, rather than in an isolated or modified training environment. Feedback, especially in these early stages, is often provided by the game itself rather than by a coach, and training becomes incrementally more difficult as players level-up and play against players of a higher rank. Perhaps because of this, again particularly in LoL, training in esports has sometimes been synonymous with playing as many games as possible as frequently as possible, otherwise known as grinding games.

The concept of specificity of learning suggests that e'athletes should engage in training practices which resemble as closely as possible to the competitive environment (Shea & Kohl, 1990). Such a view is supported by more contemporary views of motor learning and neuroscience (see Sigmundsson et al., 2017). However, the question remains whether just playing games is the optimal way to develop skill in LoL. In particular, in sport (and other domains) coaches have implemented short-cut strategies to enhance skill learning without engaging in highly demanding and time-consuming competitions. Such strategies place less physical and psychological stress on athletes and speed up the learning process.

Recognising that 'grind culture' has been prevalent in training approaches within LoL, and also that academic work on training effectiveness has been minimal, Abbott et al. (2022) set out to qualitatively explore what LoL players actually did as part of their training and how effective they perceived this training to be. In a sample of ten semi-professional and professional European players, the authors reported a consistent training pattern involved in a fairly high volume of full games:

> Players typically engaged in one or two games of "solo queue," where players "queue" into an online game typically alone and are matched with four similarly ranked teammates, upon waking up or shortly before meeting their team. Following this, four to five "scrimmage" (scrim) games are completed where the team plays in a private preorganized match against another team... After their team training, players would once again play one or two games of solo queue.
>
> (Abbott et al., 2022, p. 3)

Interestingly, players in the study by Abbott et al. (2022) were not certain as to why this standardised training structure was the norm, nor were they particularly convinced of its effectiveness. In fact, some players expressed how the pressure to play a high volume of games–due in part to the need to maintain a certain rank–at times negatively impacted their emotional well-being.

There are a number of additional and alternative training activities that can complement or supplement playing full games. At a basic level, there is a practice tool within the game client that allows an e'athlete to practise with different champions and get a feel for their abilities and movement patterns. E'athletes may also choose to create a custom game in which they are alone and can practise simply 'last hitting' minions–an opposing unit that grants gold and experience to help level-up the champion being played. Opposing champion bots can be introduced to trade (fight) against (i.e., matching damage) while maintaining a high rate of last hitting minions (sometimes referred to as creep score or CS). Interestingly, a good target is a CS of 75–80 after ten minutes. Of course it's worth noting that these training modes are individual and detached from many contextual cues that guide action in the game. Other modes available to players include 1v1, 2v2 or ARAM (All Random All Middle) games, which players predominantly use for warming-up ahead of soloQ or team scrims. Occasionally, teams might arrange to play a "blitz scrim" in which they agree to end the game after a set period of time (e.g., 14 minutes) in order to practise strategy in this phase of the game.

One key element of LoL training, and indeed many other esports games, is reviewing previous games or VODs (Video on Demand). Teams frequently review game footage of both their performances and other teams, which helps them to understand their strengths and weaknesses. Another form of development lies within watching guides published online or watching other high-ranking athletes on Twitch to understand how those athletes approach certain situations/matchups. Lastly, watching replays of games can help identify mistakes and areas for improvement. Additionally, studying professional players' gameplay can provide valuable insights into advanced strategies and techniques. In conclusion, improving at LoL requires dedication to mastering the basics, refining mechanics, effective communication with teammates, and analysing gameplay for self-improvement. However, current practice regimes seem excessive in time demands placing undue strain on the physical and psychological well-being of e'athletes.

Research has suggested that reflection, or the ability to reflect upon previous actions and performances, as part of the self-regulation process is associated with becoming an elite athlete (Jonker, 2011). As such a good way to improve gameplay is by reviewing VODs or videos of past games. However, it can be overwhelming to know where to start and how to review them effectively. The first step in reviewing VODs is to watch the game from start to finish without any distractions. This will provide a general idea of what happened during the game and where mistakes are made. After watching the entire game, an e'athlete may go back and focus on specific moments which they feel could have been played better. Another effective way to review VODs is by comparing gameplay with professional players who play the same role. This helps in identifying areas that need improvement and learn new strategies. Note-taking during VOD reviews is also important, as it creates a record of important game aspects to focus on. In conclusion, reviewing VODs is an essential part of improving gameplay in LoL. By following these tips, e'athletes can effectively review their past games and make necessary improvements for future success.

As the landscape of LoL is dynamic in nature (Watson et al., 2022), game publishers Riot Games frequently add patches to the game which change the power rankings of certain champions/items, thus changing the meta (Most Effective Tactic Available) within the game. At times, these patches can contain new champions, requiring e'athletes to understand new interactions and the abilities of the champion.

2.3   Learning a new champion in League of Legends

LoL is a complex game that requires e'athletes to master a variety of champions in order to succeed. Learning a new champion can be challenging, but there are several effective ways to do so. Firstly, it is important to read the champion's abilities and understand how they work. This approach will give the e'athlete or coach an idea of the champion's strengths and weaknesses, as well as their playstyles. Watching gameplay videos or streams of experienced e'athletes using the champion can also be helpful in understanding their mechanics. Next, practising with the champion in bot games or custom matches can help e'athletes get comfortable with the champion's abilities and combos. It is also important to experiment with different item builds and run setups to find what works best for one's particular playstyle. Finally, playing the champion in normal games with other players will allow skills to be tested against real opponents. Overall, learning a new champion requires a combination of research, practice, and experimentation.

2.4   League of Legends and patch updates

LoL, like many popular online games, undergoes regular patch updates to improve gameplay and fix bugs. Learning a new patch update can be challenging, but there are several effective ways to do it. Firstly, reading the patch notes is essential. The patch notes provide detailed information about the changes made in the update. It's important to read them thoroughly to understand how favoured champions or items have been affected. Secondly, watching professional e'athletes or streamers play on the new patch can be helpful. They often provide insights into how the changes affect gameplay and offer tips on how to adapt playstyle accordingly. Thirdly, practising in custom games or with friends can build familiarity with changes without risking a rank decrease as in ranked games. This allows e'athletes to experiment with different strategies and builds. In conclusion, learning a new patch update requires a combination of reading, watching, and practising. By utilising these methods effectively, e'athletes can stay up-to-date with the latest changes and continue improving their skills in LoL.

Patch notes are a crucial aspect of the LoL game. They are essentially a detailed list of changes made to the game by developers, which can include anything from bug fixes to balance updates and new content. These notes are released periodically, usually after major updates or patches, and provide players with an understanding of what has changed in the game. Patch notes serve several purposes in LoL. Firstly, they inform e'athletes about any changes that may affect their gameplay experience. This includes information about champion buffs or nerfs, item adjustments, and other balance changes that could impact how e'athletes approach the game. Additionally, patch notes often contain details about new features or content added to the game. This can include new champions, skins, maps, and other exciting additions that keep the game fresh and interesting for e'athletes. Overall, patch notes are an essential tool for any serious LoL player. By staying up-to-date with these updates and changes, e'athletes can adapt their strategies accordingly and stay ahead of the competition.

2.5   Training approaches in other games

2.5.1   Rocket League and custom games

Rocket League is a popular video game that requires players to control rocket-powered cars and score goals in a virtual soccer match. To become a skilled player, it is important to train and practise regularly. The first step in training for Rocket League is to understand the basic mechanics of the game, such as how the car is controlled and how to hit the ball accurately. One way to train is by playing against other players online or in local matches. This allows e'athletes to learn from their mistakes and adapt the gameplay accordingly. Another effective method is practising specific skills, such as aerial shots or dribbling, in custom games or training modes. Watching professional players' gameplay can also be helpful in improving specific skills. One can learn new strategies and techniques by observing their own gameplay and analysing their decision-making process.

One of the most challenging skills in Rocket League is aerial shots, which require players to jump and fly through the air to hit the ball. To improve their aerial shot skills, players can use custom games that focus on this specific aspect of gameplay. One of the best custom games for improving aerial shots is called "Aerial Training." This game mode allows players to practise their aerial shots by launching balls into the air at different angles and speeds. Another great custom game is "Dribbling Challenge," which helps players improve their ball control skills while in mid-air. Another popular custom game for improving aerial shots is "Obstacle Course." This game mode challenges players to navigate through an obstacle course while hitting balls in mid-air. Finally, "Freeplay" mode allows players to practise their aerial shots without any time limits or distractions. In conclusion, there are several custom games available in Rocket League that can help improve a player's aerial shot skills. By practising with these games regularly, players can become more proficient at flying through the air and scoring goals with ease.

2.5.2   *Car set-up and sim racing*

Sim racing is a popular form of motorsport that allows enthusiasts to experience the thrill of racing without leaving their homes. However, to be successful in sim racing, it is essential to have a good understanding of car set-up. Car set-up refers to the various adjustments made to a vehicle's suspension, brakes, and other components that can affect its performance on the track. To improve car set-up knowledge in sim racing, there are several steps one can take. Firstly, it is important to research and study different car set-ups used by professional racers. This will provide valuable insights into what works best for different tracks and conditions. Secondly, practising with different settings and taking note of how they affect the car's handling can help improve one's understanding of car set-up. It is also helpful to join online communities or forums where sim racers discuss their experiences and share tips on improving car set-up. Lastly, investing in high-quality equipment such as a force feedback wheel and pedals can provide more accurate feedback on how changes in car set-up affect performance on the track. By following these steps, sim racers can improve their knowledge of car set-up and ultimately become more competitive in virtual motorsport competitions.

2.6   Strategies for effective practice and performance in esports

2.6.1   *Goal-setting in league of legends*

Goal-setting is an essential aspect of success in any field, and LoL is no exception. In this popular online multiplayer game, players set goals to improve their skills and climb the ranks. The first step in goal-setting for LoL is to identify a potential long-term achievement within the game. This could be anything from reaching a certain rank or mastering a particular champion. Once this has been identified, it's important to break it down into smaller, achievable steps. For example, if the goal is to reach Diamond rank, one might set smaller goals such as improving CS or learning how to play a new role. Another important aspect of goal-setting in LoL is progress tracking. This can be done by keeping track of win/loss ratio or monitoring improvement in specific areas like CS or map awareness. In Chapter 4 the process of performance profiling is introduced. This could also be used to help identify areas to work on (this could be technical, strategical, or psychological aspects).

2.6.2 Warm-up strategies

In sport before training and competition, athletes engage in warm-up strategies to get them in the right physical and mental state to optimise learning and performance. To date very few studies have addressed this issue in sport despite the significant evidence that acute bouts of exercise can enhance cognitive (executive) functioning in children, adolescents, and adults (e.g., Ludyga et al., 2016). Moreover, low to moderate intensity exercise bouts are as effective as high intensity exercise (Moreau & Chou, 2019). In one study conducted with LoL e'athletes, it was found that a 15-minute high-intensity exercise bout on a cycle ergometer, consisting of 2.5-minute warm-up followed by 5×1-minute blocks of high intensity exercise at 80%–85% W_{peak}, interspersed with 5 blocks of low intensity exercise (40% W_{peak}) was associated with improved ability to eliminate targets (De Las Heras et al., 2020). Considering that acute bouts of exercise can lower reaction time, improve task switching and decision making (e.g., Lefferts et al., 2019), this would be a good strategy for most e'athletes to enhance their performance as well as their physical and mental well-being.

Another popular strategy in traditional sport to enhance learning and performance is the use of music. Research has shown that music has ergogenic properties, with both sedative (slow tempo, absence of strong rhythms) and functional (co-ordinated with task) music having the ability to improve cognitive functioning and motor performance, increasing positive mood, narrowing attention, and diverting attention from fatigue and pain (cognitive dissociation), enhancing the chance of achieving a flow state and alters arousal and motivation (Terry & Karageorghis, 2011). The selection of the most effective music is influenced by many factors including socio-cultural (e.g., age, gender, ethnicity, and social class) and functional aspects (such as familiarity). However, the right music, for example, can change pre-performance arousal levels by either energising or relaxing the e-athlete. The individual interpretation is important rather than musical characteristics per se in bringing about a psychophysiological response. Elliott et al. (2011) identified the internal (such as tempo, melody, and beat) and external (such as liking and familiarity) factors when selecting music for controlling anxiety and showed in a subsequent study some evidence that relaxing music was beneficial in reducing cognitive and somatic state anxiety, heart rate, and subjective relaxation

(Elliot et al., 2014). Overall, e'athletes can use music to regulate pre-performance arousal state. The choice of music should be linked to individual liking and matched to what is to be achieved (reduction in anxiety or arousal or psyching-up). In addition, music can be used in training situation to regulate mood and arousal levels and enhance attentional focus.

2.6.3   *Dietary or supplementation strategies*

The use of caffeine has been a proven strategy to enhance performance in strength and endurance events (Souza et al., 2017) and has been recommended for occupations like first responders, the military, and factory shift workers to enhance their performance (McLellan et al., 2016). Although evidence is still mixed, there is some indication that the use of caffeine prior to training or competition can enhance learning and performance. Depending on the dose, studies have shown that caffeine can enhance attentional capacity, increase alertness, and improve reaction speed and accuracy (Sainz et al., 2020).

2.7   Aim trainers in FPS

Aim training is seen to be an integral part of successful preparation in the first-person shooter (FPS) genre. Many e'athletes will utilise a form of aim trainer which simulates a firing range, allowing e'athletes to refine skills such as crosshair placement, recoil control, target selection, and accuracy.

2.7.1   *What is available for players?*

Aim trainers are custom practice-oriented play areas, developed internally or externally to the game engine where a player may compete. This can range from flash games on the internet, to custom community maps or even specific applications that provide aim training facilities. In its earliest inception, aim training was not as innovative as we know it to be now. For many, aim training was a skill practised in custom games where players would pick two points on a wall and practise 'flicking' (rapidly switching between two targets). As the games picked up popularity, individuals took it upon themselves to develop modifications that allowed specific textures to aid in aim training, or to set up custom maps where players could face-off against others in a fast-paced 1v1 gun battle.

There are a plethora of aim trainer applications available across the internet, however, Aim Labs which is available on Steam is one of the most sought-after applications for users who are looking to develop their skills. Popular FPS games such as Valorant, Call of Duty, and Counter-Strike have inbuilt 'firing ranges' which allow players to develop familiarity with the guns in the game. Popular among e'athletes, although not conventionally seen as an aim trainer, is rhythm game Osu. The objective of the game is to click, drag, and spin objects, and to successfully complete tracks, e'athletes require precise and accurate mouse movements as well as strong hand-eye coordination. E'athletes can benefit from games like Osu as it can provide the development of skills pertinent to the FPS genre while providing variety within their training environment.

2.7.2 How are aim trainers used?

Aim Labs features 12,000+ unique tasks that can allow e'athletes to practise in different contexts. It is also a highly customisable application, allowing the user to practise on the various maps as they would in the game. E'athletes can also customise the size, speed, and durability of the target. They usually split their time between practising on an aim trainer and in-game, with aim training most commonly being used as a warm-up activity for many e'athletes. Some e'athletes may even periodise their training regime to include exclusive aim training sessions, as within the FPS genre, it is arguably the most important skill for successful performance.

Aim Labs itself provides users insights to help track their development and is broken down into six components: (i) flicking, (ii) tracking, (iii) speed, (iv) precision, (v) perception, and (vi) cognition. Through a combination of these six components, e'athletes can train not only in static environments (stationary targets) to develop skills such as flicking, precision, and speed, but also in dynamic environments (moving targets) to develop their ability to track perception of objects and cognition.

2.7.3 What is the evidence for them?

Although at the time of writing, there is no objective evidence for aim trainers to be an effective tool, anecdotal evidence suggests that e'athletes do benefit from interaction with these environments. Countless professional FPS e'athletes will recount their time within aim training situations to develop their skills and may even attribute their success to the endless time spent within this environment.

Although it is important to recognise the benefit aim trainers can provide, questions can be asked on its effectiveness. Many aim training software used to this day are external to the game engine where players perform, and rarely provide dyadic interaction (player vs player). Usually, e'athletes will be practising against computer-generated targets that can move around, however will not shoot back. There can be a comparison made between aim trainers and pitching/bowling machines used by elite baseball or cricket players. Although aim trainers are more sophisticated than ball projection machines used in traditional sporting contexts, there is a degree of task de-contextualisation which may impede the direct transfer of skills from aim trainer to performance contexts (Pinder et al., 2011). By de-contextualising a task, skills and movement patterns are developed in representative means. Within the world of sports, there has always been a saying "practise how you play." Engagement within aim trainers takes away from that representativeness as e'athletes do not have to use other contextual information such as their own health points, the timing of engagement, and random movement from opponents. These points of information are crucial as it can dictate the terms of engagement, and shape how e'athletes approach certain gunfights. Representative training environments (see Bubna et al., 2023) within FPS attach consequences to errors in behaviour from players in the form of losing the gunfight.

2.7.4   How to effectively use them?

Aim trainers will yield a range of results depending on the users' proficiency within their chosen game. For novices new to the FPS genre, aim trainers can provide a sterile environment to get to grasp with mechanics required for successful aim, and calibrate settings (e.g., mouse sensitivity). For the more professional and proficient FPS e'athletes, aim trainers may not provide as much transfer as one may hope for when preparing for competition. Saying this, aim trainers can always be an effective tool to guide a warm-up routine for a professional and also be used as a tool to develop confidence in skills closer to competition/performance as the environment rewards low error rates.

To complement the use of aim trainers, professionals should take complete advantage of any deathmatch game modes within their game engine to refine their skills. Deathmatch game modes afford e'athletes opportunities to participate in gunfights at a higher frequency, allowing repetition of skills to be achieved. Gunfights are unique enough at each attempt that the application of skills are never identical, allowing for a more representative approach to development in the FPS genre.

References

Abbott, C., Watson, M., & Birch, P. (2022). Perceptions of effective training practices in League of Legends: A qualitative exploration. *Journal of Electronic, 1*, 1–11.

Blischke, K., & Erlacher, D. (2007). How sleep enhances motor learning: A review. *Journal of Human Kinetics, 17*, 3–14.

Bubna, K., Trotter, M. G., Watson, M., & Polman, R. (2023). Coaching and talent development in esports: A theoretical framework and suggestions for future research. *Frontiers in Psychology, 14*, 1–7. DOI: 10.3389/fpsyg.2023.1191801

De Las Heras, B., Li, O., Rodrigues, L., Nepveu, J.-F., & Roig, M. (2020). Exercise improves video game performance: A win-win situation. *Medicine & Science in Sports & Exercise, 52*, 1595–1602.

Elliott, D., Polman, R., & McGregor, R. (2011). Relaxing music for anxiety control. *Journal of Music Therapy, 48*, 264–288.

Elliott, D., Polman, R., & Taylor, J. (2014). The effect of relaxing music for anxiety control on competitive sport anxiety. *European Journal of Sport Science, 14*, s296–s301.

Fitts, P. M., & Posner, M. I. (1967). *Human performance*. Belmont, CA: Brooks/Cole.

Jonker, L. (2011). *Self-regulation in sport and education: Important for sport expertise and academic achievement for elite youth athletes*. The Netherlands: University of Groningen.

Lefferts, W. K., DeBlois, J. P., White, C. N., & Heffernan, K. S. (2019). Effects of acute aerobic exercise on cognition and constructs of decision making in adults with and without hypertension. *Frontiers Ageing and Neuroscience, 11*, 41.

Ludyga, S., Gerber, M., Brand, S., Holsboer-Trachsler, E., & Puhse, U. (2016). Acute effect of moderate aerobic exercise on specific aspects of executive function in different age and fitness groups: A meta-analysis. *Psychophysiology, 53*, 1611–1626.

McLellan, T. M., Caldwell, J. A., & Lieberman, H. R. (2016). A review of caffeine's effects on cognitive, physical and occupational performance. *Neuroscience and Biobehavioral Reviews, 71*, 294–312.

Miller, G. (1956). The magical number seven, plus or minus two: Some limits on our capacity for processing information. *The Psychological Review, 63*, 81–97.

Moreau, D., & Chou, E. (2019). The acute effect of high-intensity exercise on executive function: A meta-analysis. *Psychological Science, 14*, 734–764.

Pinder, R. A., Renshaw, I., Davids, K., & Kerhervé, H. (2011). Principles for the use of ball projection machines in elite and developmental sport programmes. *Sports Medicine, 41*, 793–800.

Sainz, I., Collado-Mateo, D., & Del Coso, J. (2020). Effect of acute caffeine intake on hit accuracy and reaction time in professional e-sports players. *Physiology & Behavior, 224*, 113031.

Shea, C. H., & Kohl, R. M. (1990). Specificity and variability of practice. *Research Quarterly of Exercise and Sport, 61*, 169–177.

Sigmundsson, H., Trana, L., Polman, R., & Haga, M. (2017). What is trained develops! Theoretical perspective on skill learning. *Sports, 5*, 38.

Souza, D. G., Del Coso, J., Casonattto, J., & Polito, M. D. (2017). Acute effects of caffeine-containing energy drinks on physical performance: A systematic review and meta-analysis. *European Journal of Nutrition, 56*, 13–27.

Terry, P. C., & Karageorghis, C. I. (2011). Chariots of Fire: The role of music in sport and exercise. In T. Morris & P. C. Terry (Eds.) *The new sport and exercise psychology companion*. Morgantown, WV: Fitness Information Technology.

Watson, M., Smith, D., Fenton, J., Pdraza-Ramirez, I., Laborde, S., & Cronin, C. (2022). Introducing esports coaching to sport coaching (not as sport coaching). *Sports Coaching Review*, available online ahead of print.

3 Physiological considerations for e'athletes

Craig McNulty

3.1 Introduction

Humans are a particularly adaptive species. This can be understood physiologically when a consistent *stress*, such as running or lifting weights or playing guitar, is placed upon us. We adapt, by way of improved cardiovascular fitness or developing larger and stronger muscles or forming calluses. It also occurs cognitively. Improvements in cognitive metrics such as reaction time, memory, task-switching, attention, and information processing can be seen across those that are consistently exposed to cognitively-demanding tasks or engage in regular physical exercise. Importantly, regular physical activity (PA), including exercise, is associated with improved physical and mental well-being and brain health. For example, regular PA is associated with better mood and higher levels of self-regulatory control. The latter might be particularly important in achieving goals and controlling for unwanted impulses during the competition.

Research has provided evidence of the importance of weight-based training for e'athletes (McGee & Ho, 2021), particularly in terms of injury prevention and improved posture (McGee et al., 2021; McGee & Ho, 2021; Migliore, 2021). In some cases, the positives of physiological adaptations may not be immediately apparent when considering exercise programs for e'athletes. For example, good cardiovascular fitness may not seem an important attribute for a professional e'athlete (apart from the general positive health and cognitive outcomes, of course). However, someone's ability to cope with cognitively-demanding tasks, particularly in a high-stress environment, has been linked to the efficiency of their cardiovascular system (Chang et al., 2014, 2015), with research indicating a positive association between physical fitness and cognitive performance in young adults (Åberg et al., 2009; Kohl III et al., 2013; Santana et al., 2017). To improve physical or cognitive performance, whether for health, sport, employment, or esports, there is great benefit in understanding the physiological adaptations that are specific to improving performance needs. In clinical health, understanding the needs of a patient in terms of their day-to-day activities, as well as their current limitations in relation to these activities, allows the practitioner to have greater control and direction when prescribing exercise or other activities to improve the client or patient health. This

DOI: 10.4324/9781003322382-3

is also seen in sport, where a needs analysis of the sport and player position inform physical and cognitive training programming.

The next section of this chapter will attempt to present a needs analysis of an esports title in terms of physiological and cognitive requirements. In this case, the authors have chosen League of Legends due to their own familiarity with the title – however, this concept can be adapted to any esports title. The section will outline current research in the physiological adaptations of exercise to the cardiovascular, neurological, endocrinological, and muscular systems of the body, with direct links to athlete 'needs' as identified through the needs analysis.

Note that the term 'attempt' was used, as this process is not something that is often used within professional esports team settings. Some reasons for this are discussed in Chapter 7. In addition, much like sport, or even individual positions in a sport, it is crucial that coaches address the esports needs for individual titles. The following sections of the chapter will identify several e'athletes needs that are consistent across many esports titles, however, the degree of consideration placed on these skills during training or planning should be title-dependent.

3.2   Needs analysis

League of Legends (LoL), in its flagship *Summoner's Rift* game mode, is a 5v5 multiplayer online battle arena (MOBA) game played on Microsoft Windows or Mac OS X. Each half of the map (see Figure 3.1) has a home base, along with a top, middle, and bottom 'lane'. Between the top and middle, and the middle and bottom lanes, adjacent to each base are labyrinth-type zones called the jungle. Finally, separating each team's upper and lower jungle is a top and bottom river section of the map. Each player controls a unique character, or champion. In addition to the players, the map produces a continual stream of non-player characters (NPCs) referred to as minions, as well as defensive structures called turrets. Most of the contest, or individual or team battles, occur in the lanes and jungle, as each team attempts to increase power (linked to their in-game character levels) through completing objectives and defeating their opponents (a defeated player will respawn at their base after a set period following a death). The final stages of a game will see one team (or sometimes, both) push towards the opposition's base to destroy it and win the game. Although, within a game there are several *micro-games* taking place. Examples of these include (a) lane fighting – generally a 1v1 or 2v2 battle between a player and opponent(s), (b) accumulation of gold by defeating NPCs to allow purchase of champion upgrades, (c) objective capturing, often as a team or in larger groups, such as defeating a large NPC, or destroying a turret, and (d) team fights, requiring coordinated team movement to defeat the enemy team. A game will often last 20–40 mins.

The following needs analysis is based on a single game of LoL, however, considerations will also be made for athlete fatigue as it is common for a team to play several games back-to-back in a scrimmage (training games) or during competition (best of five games, for example). In this scenario, we will not be discussing

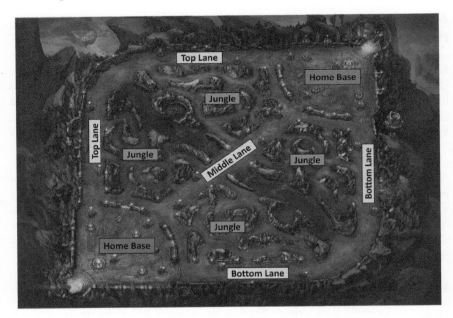

Figure 3.1 The map and play area of LoL's competitive Summoner's Rift map, including labels of the common areas of play during a game.

psychological or social needs for performance, as these will be covered in-depth in Chapters 4 and 7. However, both are important in understanding the needs of an e'athlete.

We have sub-divided the performance needs of the athlete into three categories, and further split these into specific identified needs for performance in a LoL match:

1 Operational Needs

   a Hand-eye coordination
   b Reaction time
   c Fine motor skills

2 Cognitive Needs

   a Memory
   b Strategic thinking
   c Attention
   d Task-switching
   e Information processing

3 Conditioning Needs

   a Fatigue resistance
   b Injury avoidance

3.2.1   *Operational needs*

Operational needs refer to any performance variables related to the interaction between the user and gaming hardware. In this case, between the player and the keyboard, mouse, and visual display (monitor). This includes hand to eye coordination, where the athlete will use visual on-screen cues to determine mouse and keyboard control of their champion; reaction and response time, or the e'athlete's physical and neurological ability to respond to a stimulus over a short time; and motor skills, to allow for very specific control of the e'athlete's champion and mouse pointer.

Hand to eye coordination, as well as finger coordination (fine motor skills) for keyboard inputs, and visual search are critical for performance in esports. E'athlete performance is influenced by visual function, as assessed by visual acuity, eye movement, focus, alignment, peripheral vision, and awareness (Tregel et al., 2021), which directly relates to hand to eye coordination. Compared to trained athletes (who also require high hand to eye coordination), e'athletes displayed better visual search and hand to eye coordination following complex testing across domains of perceptual-cognitive abilities (Grushko et al., 2021). Reaction time was assessed by Bickmann and colleagues (2021) across several esports genres, with comparisons drawn across sports people. They found that players of sports simulation games had shorter (improved) reaction times compared to MOBA players. No differences between e'athlete and sport athletes were found. Systematic reviews by Fernandes and colleagues (2018) and Toth and colleagues (2020) concluded that physical activity may improve reaction time, response accuracy, and working memory.

3.2.2   *Cognitive needs*

Cognitive needs are associated with cognitive functions or skills, as deemed relevant (that is, potential for performance enhancement) to a LoL game. These skills are often attributed to specific domains of cognitive brain function that assist with interpretation of external stimuli. Cognitive needs for LoL include short-term memory, such as recall of allied and opposing champion abilities; strategic thinking and cognitive flexibility to allow for adaptation to changing individual and team strategies as games evolve; attention, or maintaining focus throughout a game, which can better facilitate other cognitive processes; task-switching, which is evidenced with the need of a player to continually be shifting between lane fighting, gold accumulation, or team fighting; and information processing, which includes tracking changing game data such as player and opponent health, player gold, and mini-map movement.

In comparison to sports athletes, e'athletes performed equally well in several complex cognitive tests measuring attentional control and distribution, short-term and working spatial memory span, and reaction time (Grushko et al., 2021). Short-term memory, strategic thinking, attention, task-switching, and information processing are all cognitive skills attributed to potential improvement in esports performance (Toth et al., 2020). Naturally, these skills are improved with repetition of play, whether in a practice or a competitive setting. However, there is also opportunity to improve these skills indirectly through exercise adaptation.

Although published research on exercise and esports performance is in a stage of development, a systematic review of esports literature identified a small sample of studies which have addressed this topic. The studies indicated improved esports performance across discrete domains (such as accuracy, kill-to-death ratio, win percentage, and target elimination) during play (McNulty et al., 2023). As research in esports and physical activity is still emerging, links can be drawn from prior research which has looked at the impact of exercise on cognitive skills. These studies generally assess scores or outcomes of cognitive tests following exercise (acute and long-term). Toth and colleagues (2020) conducted an extensive dual systematic review to identify cognitive skills necessary for esports performance. Initially, the researchers identified studies which used action video games as an intervention before taking measures of performance across the cognitive domains of attention, memory, information processing, and task-switching (all of which were regarded as determinants of esports performance). The second stage of the review addressed the use of exercise interventions to assess change in cognitive skills that were previously deemed relevant to esports performance. The results concluded that exercise (which was mostly aerobic-based) has varying positive effects on sustained attention, visuospatial attention, and attentional concentration. The results of the remaining intervention studies assessing memory, information processing, and task-switching, indicated mixed results with some showing a positive correlation between exercise and cognitive performance, while others displayed no significant difference. Of the 52 intervention studies reviewed, there were none which indicated a detriment to cognitive performance following an exercise intervention. Considering the need to maintain good athlete health, which is achieved in part through physical activity, the knowledge that exercise is unlikely to cause any detriment in performance should assist coaches who currently (or plan to) incorporate physical activity as part of their athlete programming.

3.2.3   *Conditioning needs*

Conditioning needs refer to the ability to sustain an effort or action, particularly at a higher physical workload. Despite a LoL game (or many other esports titles) being undertaken entirely in a seated position, the intensity of gameplay in terms of physicality has been identified as being triple that of office workers (McGee, 2021). Two key conditioning needs for a game of LoL are fatigue resistance, or the ability for the athlete to maintain optimal physical output (in terms of actions per minute [APM] and mouse movement) for sustained periods of time; and injury avoidance, which is best achieved by conditioning the body to withstand the intense workloads. Injury avoidance can be addressed as both an acute and a long-term need.

Fatigue is a multi-dimensional concept in physiology, with several existing scientific models addressed in a review by Abbiss and Laursen (2005) that attempts to explain why we find efforts, or workloads, above what we refer to as a 'rested' state to be unmaintainable for extensive periods of time. Of course, our ability to resist fatigue is dependent on the workload in relation to our 'fitness'. That is, a sedentary or an untrained individual and a highly-trained endurance cyclist or a runner will both reach a state of fatigue when undertaking a sustained workload above rested. The obvious difference being the intensity of the workload required to approach fatigue for each of these individuals. A cardiovascular fit individual can maintain homeostasis at a much higher energy output. For simplicity, we will consider fatigue in terms of the cardiovascular, metabolic energy, and neuromuscular systems models (Noakes, 2000). Psychological, or motivational fatigue, will be addressed in Chapter 4.

During a sustained effort across a single or multiple game(s), an e'athlete will average 500–600 APM (McGee, 2021). As well, due to cognitive efforts discussed earlier, e'athletes maintain an increased cardiac output (heart rate [HR]) for the duration of the game(s). HR data for an elite LoL athlete is presented in Figure 3.2. The data displays both the 'at rest' HR and during a ranked LoL match.

As can be seen in Figure 3.2, the HR during gameplay and at rest indicates a significant increase in cardiac output during play. Leis and colleagues (2022) presented HR data of a group of LoL athletes competing in a practice scrimmage and in a competitive format. For the same group of e'athletes, HR was increased during the competitive match (see Figure 3.3), which may be attributed to individual stress responses. HR increases in response to the need for oxygen delivery to peripheral tissue (such as working muscle), the transport of metabolic by-products (such as carbon dioxide and lactate – not to be mistaken with lactic acid). It also increases in response to perceived stress, which we often refer to as the *flight or fight* response, and is understandably elicited during a competitive LoL game where alertness and quick decision-making are essential. Firstly, the ability of the cardiovascular system to deliver oxygen and remove waste products is entirely dependent on its efficiency, which improves as an adaptation to cardiovascular exercise (Hellsten & Nyberg, 2015). Exercise which stresses the cardiovascular system, such as running, cycling, or swimming, will trigger adaptations such as (1) increased red blood cell count along with improved oxygen-carrying capacity of haemoglobin (the oxygen transport molecule), (2) increased capillary density,

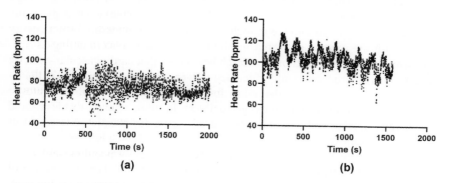

Figure 3.2 Raw HR data of elite e'athlete collected during seated rest (above), and raw HR data collected from the same e'athlete during a ranked LoL match (below). Note the variations in heart rate are more prominent during the ranked match, and likely in response to different match stimuli (such as team battles).

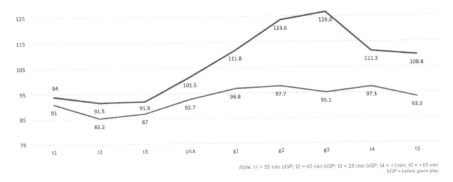

Figure 3.3 Data presented by Leis et al. (2022) of the mean HR differences between a group of LoL athletes during training and during competition. The time stamps indicate: t1–55 mins prior to game play; t2–40 mins prior to game play; t3–25 mins prior to gameplay; pick – champion selection; g1–5 mins into game; g2 – final 10 mins of game; g3 – final 5 mins of game; t4 – 1 min after game; t5–15 mins after game; and t6–30 mins after game.

particularly relating to the working muscle, improving blood vessel to tissue surface area and therefore oxygen diffusion, and (3) increased volume of blood being pumped by the heart.

Cardiovascular efficiency (fitness) is dependent on not only oxygen delivery but also oxygen uptake at a cellular level within exercising muscle. Metabolic energy demand refers to the cellular requirement of substrates (such as carbohydrates and fats) and enzymatic processes which convert substrates to a useable form of energy for sustained muscular action. Homeostasis (or, equilibrium of energy requirements and conversion of substrates to energy to meet the requirements) and therefore fatigue resistance rely on the cell's ability to transport and utilise oxygen from the blood into the cell's mitochondria. The cell converts simple substrates such as glucose (wherein, energy is stored within the molecular bonds) to energy (in the form of adenosine triphosphate, or ATP), or to molecules such as pyruvate. Pyruvate can be shuttled into the mitochondria of a cell to undergo further energy transfer, with the oxygen delivered by the cardiovascular system acting as a final pathway for ATP production. Research has shown that cardiovascular exercise improves energy production and efficiency (Rivera-Brown & Frontera, 2012) by increasing metabolic enzymes that allow for increased conversion of substrates to ATP, as well as improved cellular oxygen delivery. In sports science, this is referred to as oxygen uptake, and is a commonly used metric for indirect assessment of cardiovascular fitness.

The neuromuscular system encompasses the nervous system and muscular system, and more specifically the communication between them. The cooperation of these two systems relies on chemical interactions at the neuromuscular junction. Whether initiated at the premotor cortex in the brain (for voluntary muscular action) or at the spinal cord (involuntary muscular action), information is passed through the nerves via an action potential. On reaching the neuromuscular junction, the information will be transferred to the muscle via neurotransmitters (primarily acetylcholine). These neurotransmitters bind to receptors of the muscle, creating a new action potential which is regulated by ionic gates within the cell. The following process which leads to muscular contraction involves the movement of ions across the cell wall, and the 'splitting' of ATP molecules for energy transfer for contraction. Physical activity has been shown to improve the synergy of the neurological and muscular system interactions (Deschenes, 2019). This is particularly evident when the exercises replicate the activity. In a sport like football, the ability to kick a ball accurately and powerfully during a free kick or corner requires further physical adaptation than just muscular power. It requires a very specific and organised contraction of muscle during the kick motion. This neuromuscular synergy is achieved in football in part through the repetitive practice of kicking a ball, as well as technical improvements through coaching. In esports, the use of software such as Aim Lab (aimlab.gg), has been thought to replicate the discrete muscular movements needed to improve gameplay. However, it should be noted that there is currently no strong evidence to support the use of Aim Lab for enhancing performance in FPS titles.

Even for readers unacquainted with the biological sciences, it should be fast becoming obvious how important the interactions of these systems become in terms of allowing work (physical effort) to be undertaken efficiently. Not dissimilar to complex machines, dysfunction or inefficiencies in discrete parts of the machine can quickly create bottlenecks in the larger system. Fatigue becomes apparent when one or more of these systems are unable to match the physical demands in place. Abbott and colleagues (2023) interviewed ten professional LoL athletes across Europe to gain insight into the athlete's perceptions of their training workload and associated fatigue. The interviews concluded a strong awareness from athletes that the common professional training structure, or 'grind culture', is inducive to fatigue and athlete burnout. The degree of control an athlete or coach has on their competitive roster is limited, however fatigue over multiple games may be attenuated through physical preparation of the cardiovascular, metabolic, and neuromuscular systems. Exercises that replicate the needs of an athlete during competition will promote positive adaptation to improve fatigue resistance. Running, for example, will improve cardiovascular efficiency and metabolic responses which has been shown to improve regulation of HR during competitive matches (Nicholson et al., 2020).

The ability to match the physical demands of esports also needs to be considered in terms of injury prevention. Elite LoL athletes perform repetitive fine motor movements, through keyboard and mouse control, for an average of 5.5–10 hours per day as they approach competition (DiFrancisco-Donoghue et al., 2019), while maintaining an upright seated position. This workload places e'athletes at an increased risk of wrist/hand and postural (neck and back) injury or pain (McGee, 2021). DiFrancisco-Donoghue and colleagues (2019) surveyed 65 collegiate e'athletes (18–22 years) and found that 42% reported neck or back pain, 36% reported wrist pain, and 32% reported hand pain at some point in their careers. The e'athletes reported that they practised between 5.5 and 10 hours per day. Migliore

(2021) noted several premature retirements of professional e'athletes due to injury, which included many in their early 20s, and even late teens, retiring due to overuse hand and wrist-related injury. Injuries are not uncommon in sport, where many professional athletes undergo periods of missed games due to injury, with some requiring surgery before the eventual return to the sport. And like esports, some athletes are unable to return to their sport (at least not at the same competitive level) due to severe (often referred to as 'career ending') injury. However, there is currently a much higher focus on injury prevention and rehabilitation in professional sport in general, compared to esports. Longevity of the athlete's career, as well as the team/management's desire to have the athlete back to full capacity, are factors that have influenced a strong culture of injury knowledge, prevention, and management in sport. Of the e'athletes surveyed by DiFrancisco and colleagues (2019), only 2% sought medical treatment for an injury. Migliore (2021) discussed potential issues within the 'injury culture' of esports. Although a keen awareness of potential injury risk exists, there is a general lack of emphasis on injury prevention. As well, e'athletes and coaches are not particularly reactive when an injury does occur.

The science of injury prevention and rehabilitation for a variety of esports-related injuries are well-established (Amini, 2011). Increasing muscular and joint strength, mobility and endurance of the hands, wrists, back, and neck will allow for greater avoidance of injury. For example, an e'athlete that undertakes consistent (several sessions per week) upper extremity strengthening exercises, will likely see a decrease in future injury risk. In addition, if an injury were to occur, the e'athlete is in a better physical position to alleviate symptoms or return to play sooner. Strength exercises which replicate the movements and activities of the lower limb will have the greatest positive impact. Performing mobility exercises, will allow for a greater degree of safe movement during play, particularly over extended periods. Diminished strength and mobility are two key risk factors for injury, and addressing these as part of a standard physical training program should be included for training of all e'athletes. Similarly, consistent muscular strength and endurance training of the postural muscles of the neck and back will condition e'athletes for the lengthy periods spent in an upright and seated position.

Aside from fatigue resistance and injury prevention, emerging research has shown that physical activity may play an important role in e'athlete performance as well as perceived performance (McNulty et al., 2023). Additionally, the need for heightened cognitive function, fine motor skills, and hand to eye coordination for esports performance is clear. The positive impact of exercise and cognitive-specific training on athlete cognition, coordination, and conditioning should encourage e'athletes and coaches to incorporate consistent exercise training within their standard weekly schedules. The benefits of this extend further than performance, as e'athlete health and well-being are improved with regular physical activity. Of course, mental well-being of e'athletes in a competitive esports environment is also a determinant of an e'athlete's health and career longevity, and this will be discussed in the following chapter.

3.3   Physiological measures to inform esports performance and health

Understanding how physical activity, exercise, and cognitive training may impact esports performance and health is important. Likewise, being able to measure and track these variables will allow for greater insight in to e'athlete programming. There are numerous measurable physiological variables which may apply to esports performance. Of course, many of these measures, or tests, require qualified practitioners and/or expensive equipment. Thankfully, most variables as they apply to sports physiology, have multiple means of measurement with varying degrees of validity. For example, in sports science, cardiovascular endurance performance (such as long distance running or swimming) may be indirectly measured using a series of expired gas analysers (i.e. oxygen, carbon dioxide, and nitrogen), where expired breath from the subject is passed through a ventilation turbine, into the gas analysers, and the results often produced live and digitally on a connected device or computer. These indirect calorimetry systems range in price from thousands to hundreds of thousands of $USD. These systems, although still using an indirect method of measurement, are considered the most valid devices for measuring energy expenditure or expired gas (which is used to accurately predict cardiovascular fitness). Although, another physiological measure of cardiovascular fitness is HR. HR monitoring devices are significantly cheaper, given how commonplace these devices have become in smart watches, exercise equipment, and wearable devices such as chest straps. Despite the notable difference in price, the use of HR (generally via HR monitors) to measure cardiovascular fitness and predict performance is highly valid (Achten & Jeukendrup, 2003). Expired gas analysis, HR, heart rate variability, and fatigue assessment are all important measures which may inform e'athlete programming for performance and health.

Before further discussing some of the key physiological measures of performance, we should confirm our understanding of the terms direct and indirect measurements, test validity, and test reliability. Understanding these concepts will greatly inform test selection.

The terms *direct* and *indirect* in physiological testing refer to the variable of interest, and if any assumptions are to be drawn from the variable. That is, a direct measure is one which measures exactly the variable of interest. Stature and mass are common examples of direct measurements. If you wanted to know how tall an individual was in centimetres, you could use a tape measure or stadiometer to directly measure their height in centimetres. HR is another direct measure, however, we will discuss this shortly. An indirect measure refers to the use of surrogate markers to estimate a variable where direct measurement may not be possible. Often the measured variable is used within a predictive formula, or used as a basis of assumption on the expected outcome of another variable. Examples of indirect measurements in physiology include the use of blood pressure as an indicator of cardiovascular health, or the use of HRV to estimate autonomic nervous system activity.

Validity in physiological testing refers to the degree (often presented in research as a value between -1 and $+1$) in which a test accurately measures the physiological parameter it intends to measure. In research, often tests are assessed for their validity by comparing the measures of the test to a 'gold standard' measure or reference. For example, skinfold thickness, waist circumference, and body mass index are all indirect measures of body composition. The validity of these measures all differ, and their validity has been ascertained through study comparisons to a gold standard measure such as magnetic resonance imaging (MRI) or duel X-ray absorptiometry (DEXA) scanning. As you may have guessed, MRI and DEXA scanning systems are something likely to be only found in research institutes and hospitals, and require specialist staff to operate. Therefore, having more accessible forms of body composition measures available is necessary, even at the loss of some validity.

Reliability in physiological tests refers to the degree to which a test produces consistent and repeatable results over time and across different testing conditions. These results are normally statistically expressed as a value ranging from 0 (no reliability) to 1 (perfect reliability), where values of 0.8 or above are generally considered highly reliable. A reliable test should yield similar results when administered to the same individual at different times or by different examiners. Reliability may be affected by equipment calibration (or lack of), novice assessors, or uncontrolled external influences (such as a subject drinking a large quantity of water prior to a body composition test versus being tested while fasted).

Validity and reliability should be understood for all physiological testing. Most common tests of performance (such as cardiovascular fitness, strength, and cognitive skills) will have published research addressing the validity and reliability of the test. Some advice for searching for published research assessing either the validity or reliability of a test includes noting the population used in the study and the sample size. The population used, where possible, should closely represent the target group a practitioner is planning to test. For example, there may be research on a specific test used in an esports population. However, as this research may not exist, a similar population group may be as informative (such as those which are mostly seated but require increased cognition and stress mitigation, such as race car drivers or pilots). The sample size, that is the number of participants used in the study, should also be considered. The rule of thumb is that a larger sample size will give more confidence to the results. Again, with esports physiology research still in its infancy, reliance on other similar subject groups where more data is available may be necessary.

3.3.1 *Expired gas analysis*

Expired gas analysis, or indirect calorimetry, is a valuable tool in sports physiology that can be used to indirectly assess an athlete's cardiovascular endurance capacity. By measuring the levels of oxygen and carbon dioxide in an athlete's expired breath, this analysis can provide insight into the efficiency of their aerobic metabolism and the level of exertion they are experiencing during exercise. This information can be used to develop customised training programs that optimise an e'athlete's cardiovascular capacity and improve their overall performance. Additionally, expired gas analysis can be used to monitor the effects of altitude training, assess an e'athlete's recovery from injury, and diagnose exercise-induced asthma or other respiratory conditions that may impact athletic performance. There is limited research in the use of expired gas analysis in esports performance (Nicholson et al., 2023a, 2023b; Zimmer et al., 2022), however its use in sports science research has been ongoing for a century. Two key physiological performance variables that can be acquired through expired gas analysis are oxygen uptake and ventilation threshold (obtained by a ventilation metre).

Oxygen uptake refers to the amount of molecular oxygen (the primary catalyst for aerobic energy output) that is utilised within the cells of the body. This measure can be viewed as an assessment of cardiovascular efficiency. For example, a highly trained endurance athlete would have a larger range of oxygen utilisation than an untrained individual. This means that at rest, an endurance athlete would require less oxygen to maintain homeostasis, and similarly could utilise more than a non-trained subject at higher intensities. This is all due to their improved cardiovascular efficiency as an adaptation to training. A larger range of oxygen uptake, as well as a higher value at peak oxygen uptake (for example, during a high intensity exercise test), is a strong indicator of endurance performance.

Ventilation threshold refers to the point during exercise where the demand for oxygen exceeds the supply that the cardiovascular system can deliver. This results in an increase in the concentration of carbon dioxide in the blood, which triggers an autonomic reflex response to increase breathing rate. It is likely you have experienced this yourself, as hyperventilation, on reaching a higher intensity of exercise. Ventilation threshold is highly trainable and will improve as an adaptation to exercise to allow for sustained efforts of higher intensities of exercise. Figure 3.4

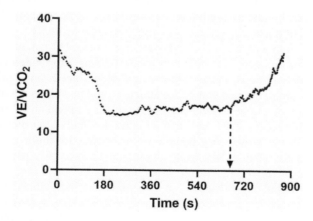

Figure 3.4 Data collected from a participant completing an incremental maximal test to exhaustion. By graphing ventilation data over expired carbon dioxide, the participant's ventilation threshold can be identified as the point in which the data transitions from a linear function (noted by the hashed arrow). A practitioner can calculate the intensity of exercise at this timepoint, and use that intensity as a threshold for sub-maximal and supra-maximal exercise.

displays ventilation over expired carbon dioxide data from an incremental maximal exercise test. The point at which data transitions from a linear function is indicative of ventilation threshold.

Expired gas analysis devices are commonplace in well-resourced sports science centres, health clinics, or athlete institutes, however their price tag often limits their use privately or within clubs and institutes with more restricted finances. As well, a qualified and experienced practitioner is required to operate the equipment and accurately interpret the results. Therefore, coaches or e'athletes interested in attaining oxygen uptake data should get in contact with local sporting institutes or physiology centres.

3.3.2   *Electrocardiography (ECG) and photoplethysmography (PPG)*

ECG and PPG are non-invasive technologies that can be used to measure physiological performance variables of cardiac function such as HR and HRV. ECG measures electrical activity of the heart, such as that which occurs during a cardiac cycle (a heartbeat). As muscle contracts when electrically stimulated, many inferences can be made about the heart function by measuring the electrical activity. ECG technology is most seen in chest strap HR monitors or other similar wearable devices. PPG measures changes in blood volume in the skin using light. PPG sensors emit light into the skin and measure the amount of light that is reflected back to the device. Blood absorbs light, so changes in blood volume can be detected by changes in the amount of reflected light. PPG sensors are often used in wearable devices such as smartwatches. Key variables for performance that can be obtained from ECG and PPG are HR, HR deflection, and HRV.

HR is a commonly used physiological measure in sports science that provides valuable information about an athlete's cardiovascular function and fitness level. By monitoring HR during exercise, or as a variable during exercise testing, coaches can gain insight into an e'athlete's cardiovascular fitness. HR can also be used to determine fatigue and general health and wellness. This information can be used to tailor training programs to an e'athlete's individual needs and optimise their performance. A highly trained endurance athlete would be able to maintain higher exercise intensity output at a lower percentage of their maximal HR (determined biologically, and recedes with age) than an untrained individual. For example, a trained long-distance runner may be able to maintain a 16 km/hr running speed at say 75% of their maximal HR, while an untrained person may require an effort of 95% of their maximal HR. The closer an individual's HR is to their biological maximum (approximately calculated as 220 minus the individuals age in years) at a set exercise intensity, the sooner they will reach fatigue if continuing at that intensity. As the body adapts to endurance exercise, the HR should progressively lower (over weeks and months) for a set intensity. As mentioned, HR can be used to determine intensity and duration of exercise when programming for an athlete. Figure 3.5 displays HR data following an incremental maximal exercise test, as well as the same data fit with two linear functions, with the point of intersection indicating the HR deflection point. Although HR deflection and ventilation threshold

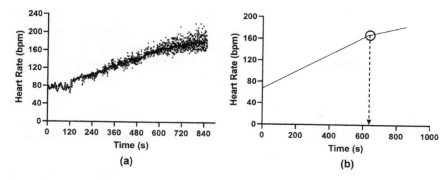

Figure 3.5 Raw HR data from a maximal incremental exercise test to exhaustion (a), and the same data set fit with two linear regressions, where the point of intersection indicates the HR deflection point (b).

are two unique phenomena, they both occur at similar timepoints that align with the individual's inability to maintain homeostasis (or, the point at which energy can no longer be produced at the same rate of demand during exercise).

HR deflection refers to the point during exercise where HR begins to level off or decrease, despite an increase in the exercise intensity. This phenomenon is similar to the ventilation threshold in that it occurs as a result of the body's shift from aerobic to anaerobic energy production (discussed further in Chapter 5), as increased oxygen demand can no longer be met. HR deflection can be determined using collected HR data during an incremental exercise test. Like the ventilation threshold, HR deflection is highly trainable and a strong indicator of what intensity an athlete will perceive as moderate (below threshold) or vigorous (above threshold).

HRV is a measure of the variation in time between heartbeats and is increasingly being used in sports science to assess an athlete's physiological response to training and competition. By analysing changes in HRV, trainers can gain insight into an athlete's autonomic nervous system activity, stress levels, and readiness to perform. This information can be used to develop customised training programs that optimise an athlete's performance, prevent overtraining, and reduce the risk of injury. Additionally, HRV monitoring can be used to identify early signs of fatigue, illness, or other factors that may impact an athlete's ability to perform at their best. HRV data is relatively simple to collect with a HR monitor or similar device, and can be easily calculated using HR data. However, correctly interpreting HRV data takes knowledge and experience, and caution should be taken when implementing changes to training based on HRV.

As mentioned previously, physiological measures during (simulated) esports practice and competition is still in an early growth phase. A review by Koshy and Koshy (2020) addressed the use of ECG as a method to physiologically monitor e'athletes. As well, some prior research has attempted to quantify HR and HRV response to esports competition. HR and HRV were collected pre-, during, and post-competition in 14 collegiate-aged male members of the University of Mississippi esports team (Andre et al., 2020). The study reported mean HR during competition were significantly elevated compared to mean pre-competition values (131.4 ± 19.0 bpm vs. 97.1 ± 19.9 bpm). Peak HR during competition (188.1 ± 32.9 bpm) were also significantly elevated compared to pre-competition values of 119.6 ± 20.1. This is a 57% increase in peak HR, and a 35% increase in mean HR while essentially seated and 'inactive'. The increase in cardiovascular response to esports competition may be attributed to a physiological stress response (Andre et al., 2020). Interestingly, a study by Watanabe and colleagues (2021), which measured the HR response by ECG of nine professional Street Fighter V e'athletes, showed a higher mean HR when versing another human player (98 bpm) compared to versing the computer AI (86 bpm) and at baseline (79 bpm).

It seems clear from preliminary research that there is a relationship between esports competition and a cardiovascular response. From the perspective of stress mitigation and maintenance of optimal arousal during competition, it is important to have an understanding of the cardiovascular response of e'athletes as well as methods to physiologically and psychologically (discussed in depth in Chapter 4) prepare an athlete.

3.3.3 Fatigue resistance

Fatigue was introduced earlier in this chapter as a multi-dimensional concept supported by several scientific models. We discussed physiological fatigue resistance as a determinant of an individual's fitness in terms of maintaining homeostasis during increased intensities of work, and conditioning such as adaptations to chronic workloads (for example, back-to-back competitive esports matches). Fatigue resistance is critical to performance at high levels of esports. The ability to resist fatigue is determined by a combination of factors including muscular strength, endurance, aerobic capacity, and recovery ability. Additionally, the use of nutritional strategies, such as carbohydrate loading and hydration, can also enhance an athlete's ability to resist fatigue and perform at a high level for extended periods of time. We will discuss nutritional interventions in depth in Chapter 5.

In sport, fatigue monitoring may involve a variety of measures including athlete-self report (such as sleep, stress, and mood), autonomic nervous system measures (such as HR and HRV responses), physical performance (depending on the sport, these may include repeated sprints or maximal muscular contractions), neuromuscular function (such as counter movement jumps and other high acceleration exercises), joint range of motion (such as hips and shoulders), and hormonal responses (such as measures of creatine-kinase and uric acid) (Thorpe et al., 2017). Some of these measures can be utilised with an esports population. Athlete self-report or non-invasive measures can be conducted on a regular or daily basis, such as during training or heavy competition schedules. Some commonly used questionnaires are described as follows:

1 The Profile of Mood States (POMS): The POMS is a widely used questionnaire that assesses various dimensions of mood, including tension, depression, anger, vigour, fatigue, and confusion.

2 The Recovery-Stress Questionnaire for Athletes (RESTQ-Sport): The RESTQ-Sport is a questionnaire that measures the balance between an athlete's recovery and stress levels. It assesses factors such as general stress, emotional stress, social stress, physical stress, and fatigue.

3 The Athlete Sleep Screening Questionnaire (ASSQ): The ASSQ is a questionnaire that assesses an athlete's sleep quality and quantity. It assesses factors such as sleep duration, sleep quality, sleep latency, and sleep disturbances.

4 The Daily Analysis of Life Demands of Athletes (DALDA): The DALDA is a questionnaire that assesses an athlete's daily demands and stressors, such as training and competition demands, as well as psychological stressors such as pressure and social stress.

5 The Recovery Cue Checklist (RCC): The RCC is a questionnaire that assesses an athlete's recovery status. It assesses factors such as hydration, nutrition, sleep quality, stress levels, and mood.

Of course, undertaking all of these questionnaires on a daily or regular basis would be time consuming. Esports practitioners may wish to create their own custom questionnaire incorporating aspects of the above commonly used surveys most appropriate to their esport and e'athlete needs. It's important to remember that when altering/customising an existing questionnaire, there may be some loss in validity.

References

Abbiss, C. R., & Laursen, P. B. (2005). Models to explain fatigue during prolonged endurance cycling. *Sports Medicine, 35*, 865–898.

Abbott, C., Watson, M., & Birch, P. (2023). Perceptions of effective training practices in League of Legends: a qualitative exploration. *Journal of Electronic Gaming and Esports, 1*, 1–11.

Åberg, M. A. I., Pederson, N. L., Torén, K., Svartengren, M., Bäckstrtand, B., Johnsson, T., Cooper-Khun, C. M., Åberg, N. D., Nilsson, M., & Kuhn, H. G. (2009). Cardiovascular fitness is associated with cognition in young adulthood. *The Proceedings of the National Academy of Scienes, 106*, 20906–20911.

Achten, J., & Jeukendrup, A. E. (2003). Heart rate monitoring: applications and limitations. *Sports Medicine, 33*, 517–538.

Aimlab. (2022). Aimlab. https://aimlab.gg/

Amini, D. (2011). Occupational therapy interventions for work-related injuries and conditions of the forearm, wrist, and hand: a systematic review. *The American Journal of Occupational Therapy, 65*, 29–36.

Andre, T. L., Walsh, S. M., Valladão, S., & Cox, D. (2020). Physiological and perceptual response to a live collegiate esports tournament. *International Journal of Exercise Science, 13*(6), 1418–1429.

Bickmann, P., Wechsler, K., Rudolf, K., Tholl, C., Froböse, I., & Grieben, C. (2021). Comparison of reaction time between esports players of different genres and sportsmen. *International Journal of Esports Research, 1*, 1–16.

Chang, Y., Chi, L., Etnier, J. L., Wang, C., Chu, C., & Zhou, C. (2014a). Effect of acute aerobic exercise on cognitive performance: role of cardiovascular fitness. *Psychology of Sport and Exercise, 15*, 464–470.

Chang, Y., Chu, C., Wang, C., Song, T., & Wei, G. (2015). Effect of acute exercise and cardiovascular fitness on cognitive function: an event-related cortical desynchronization study. *Psychophysiology, 52*, 342–351.

Deschenes, M. R. (2019). Adaptations of the neuromuscular junction to exercise training. *Current Opinion in Physiology, 10*, 10–16.

DiFrancisco-Donoghue, J., Balentine, J., Schmidt, G., & Zwibel, H. (2019). Managing the health of the esport athlete: an integrated health management model. *Sport & Exercise Medicine, 5*, 1–6.

Fernandes, R. M., Correa, M. G., dos Santos, M. A. R., Almeida, A. P. C. P. S. C., Fagundes, N. C. F., Maia, L. C., & Lima, R. R. (2018). The effects of moderate physical exercise on adult cognition: a systematic review. *Frontiers in Physiology, 9*, 1–11.

Grushko, A., Morozova, O., Ostapchuk, M., & Korobeynikova, E. (2021). Perceptual-cognitive demands of esports and team sports: a comparative study. *Advances in Cognitive Research, Artificial Intelligence and Neuroinformatics, 1358*, 36–43.

Hellsten, Y., & Nyberg, M. (2015). Cardiovascular adaptations to exercise training. *Comprehensive Physiology, 6*, 1–32.

Kohl III, H., W., & Cook, H. D. (2013). Committee on physical activity and physical education in the school environment. In Food and Nutrition Board; Institute of Medicine (Eds.). Educating the student body: Taking physical activity and physical education to school. National Academies Press, Washington, D.C.

Koshy, A., & Koshy, G. M. (2020). The potential of physiological monitoring technologies in esports. *International Journal of Esports, 1*(1), 1–11.

League of Legends Wiki. (n.d.). https://leagueoflegends.fandom.com/wiki/Map_(League_of_Legends).

Leis, O., Pedraza-Ramirez, I., Demirsöz, G., Watson, M., Laborde, S., Elbe, A.-M., & Lautenbach, F. (2022, July 13). Psychophysiological stress in esports settings: training vs. competition. In O. Leis (Chair). *Applications of Sport Psychology to esports: Insights into health and performance research.* 16th European Congress of Sport and Exercise Psychology, Padua, Italy.

McGee, C., & Ho, K. (2021). Tendinopathies in video gaming and esports. *Frontiers in Sports and Active Living, 3*, 1–4.

McGee, C., Hwu, M., Nicholson, L. L., & Ho, K. K. N. (2021). More than a game: musculoskeletal injuries and a key role for the physical therapist in esports. *Journal of Orthopaedic & Sports Physical Therapy, 51*, 415–472.

McNulty, C., Jenny, S. E., Leis, O., Poulus, D., Sondergeld, P., & Nicholson, M. (2023). Physical exercise and performance in esports players: an initial systematic review. *Journal of Electronic Gaming and Esports, 1*(1), 1–11..

Migliore, L. (2021). Prevention of esports injuries. In L. Migliore, C. McGee, & M. N. Moore (Eds.), *Handbook of Esports Medicine: Clinical Aspects of Competitive Video Gaming*, pp. 213–240. Springer Link.

Nicholson, M., Poulus, D., & McNulty, C. (2020). Letter in response to review: more physiological research is needed in esports. *International Journal of Esports, 1*, 1–6.

Nicholson, M., Poulus, D., Roberts, R., Kelly, V., & McNulty, C. (2023a). *Quantifying energy expenditure and HRV within elite esports.* Unpublished manuscript.

Nicholson, M., Roberts, R., Poulus, D., Johnson, D., Kelly, V., & McNulty, C. (2023b). *What is the impact of an exercise intervention on cognitive function within League of Legends players? An fNIRS study.* Unpublished manuscript.

Noakes, T. D. (2000). Physiological models to understand exercise fatigue and the adaptations that predict or enhance athletic performance. *Scandinavian Journal of Medicine and Science in Sports, 10*, 123–145.

Rivera-Brown, A. M., & Frontera, W. R. (2012). Principles of exercise physiology: responses to acute exercise and long-term adaptations to training. *PM&R, 4*, 797–804.

Santana, C. C. A., Azevedo, L. B., Cattacuzzo, M. T., Hill, J. O., Andrade, L. P., & Prado, W. L. (2017). Physical fitness and academic performance in youth: a systematic review. *Scandanavian Journal of Medicine & Science in Sports, 27*, 579–603.

Thorpe, R. T., Atkinson, G., Drust, B., & Gregson, W. (2017). Monitoring fatigue status in elite team-sport athletes: implications for practice. *International Journal of Sports Physiology and Performance, 12*(2), S227–S234.

Toth, A. J., Ramsbottom, N., Kowal, M., & Campbell, M. J. (2020). Converging evidence supporting the cognitive link between exercise and esport performance: a dual systematic review. *Brain Sciences, 10*, 1–34.

Tregel, T., Sarpe-Tudoran, T., Müller, P. N., & Göbel, S. (2021). Analyzing game-based training methods for selected esports titles in competitive gaming. In B. Fletcher, M. Ma, S. Göbel, J Baalsrud Hauge, & T. Marsh (Eds.), *Lecture Notes in Computer Science*, pp. 213–228. Springer.

Watanabe, K., Saijo, N., Minami, S., & Kashino, M. (2021). The effects of competitive and interactive play on physiological state in professional esports players. *Heliyon, 7*(4), 1–7.

Zimmer, R. T., Haupt, S., Heidenreich, H., & Schmidt, W. F. J. (2022). Acute effects of esports on the cardiovascular system and energy expenditure in amateur esports players. *Frontiers of Sports and Active Living, 11*(4), 1–9.

4 Psychological considerations for esports athletes

Remco Polman

4.1 Introduction

In this book, we consider individuals engaged in esports as athletes. We know that psychological factors play a considerable role in the success of athletes in traditional sports. There is an abundance of research and empirical findings which have provided insights into psychological factors which influence performance and to a lesser extent psychological interventions which help athletes build psychological skills to succeed or to deal with negative psychological experiences like fear of failure, state anxiety, or low self-confidence. In this chapter, we discuss the current limited research on the psychological factors influencing esports performance as well as highlight concepts from performance and sports psychology which we think are relevant to e'athletes to enhance both their performance and well-being.

4.2 Stress and coping

4.2.1 Stress response

An important factor influencing any performance is the experience of stress. Hence, stress influences your ability to conduct academic exams, execute motor skills, or a job interview. Stress is also a major concern in esports and has been shown to affect e'athletes' health and well-being across all levels (Madden & Harteveld, 2021). We will provide a simple example of how stress influences performance at multiple levels. If you would be asked to walk over a 10-meter long and 20-cm wide wooden beam lying on the floor, most of us would have no problem doing this successfully. However, if the same wooden beam is suspended 5 meters in the air, some of us would not even consider walking over it. In addition, if we decided to give it a go, the way the task is executed is likely to differ dramatically from when you would walk on it when the beam is located on the floor.

It is not that the task has suddenly become more difficult. The main difference is that you now start thinking about the potential consequences of dropping of the beam (like you are thinking about the consequences of making mistakes when competing in your esports). For most of us, this creates significant levels of stress, fear, and state anxiety. Consequently, the way we approach the task is very different.

DOI: 10.4324/9781003322382-4

Anxiety, for example, results in changes in your heart rate and breathing patterns. Regarding the latter, when feeling more anxious, your breathing is likely to become shallower in nature (breathing from the chest rather than the abdomen), increasing CO_2 concentration in your body. These increased levels of CO_2, in turn, increase your levels of stress, fear, and state anxiety further whilst increasing heart rate and blood pressure. Importantly, the increased levels of CO_2 in your body because of the altered breathing pattern will also influence cognitive functioning negatively impairing your decision-making capabilities. Concurrently there is likely to be more co-contraction of muscles in your body. This will result in slower, more rigid, and unstable movement patterns. The same consequences would apply to athletes performing in esports. When stressed, they are more likely to show slow and impaired decision-making and respond slower and inaccurately to events.

This simple example shows that the way we respond to a stressor has several and varied outcomes. These can be classified as psychological (e.g., state anxiety and fear), behavioural (e.g., smoothness of motor execution; speed and coordination), cognitive (e.g., intrusive and repetitive thoughts), and physiological (e.g., co-contracting of muscles, breathing, heart rate, and cortisol response). As indicated in Figure 4.1, the source of stress can also be varied and originate from multiple domains.

4.2.2 Stressor type

Stress is what you think it is. It is your interpretation and reaction to events. Hence, competing in a League of Legends (LoL) competition in front of 10,000 spectators can be very threatening for some but neutral or even exciting for others. It is when the demands of the situation exceed your resources to react adaptively that e'athletes will experience stress. As indicated in Figure 4.1, the sources of stress are varied and the way we interpret them are dependent on factors like your personality, age, and gender. In one of the first studies on the sources of stress experienced by e'athletes competing in either DOTA2, LoL, CS:GO, Overwatch

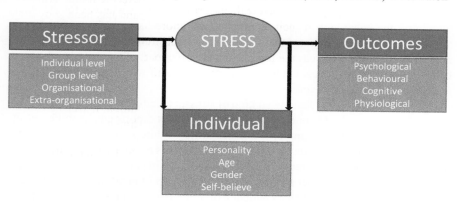

Figure 4.1 The stress response.

or Rainbow Six Siege, the authors identified five major themes: (1) performance, (2) teammate, (3) external individuals, (4) balancing life commitments, and (5) technical issues (Poulus et al., 2022a). These categories are not dissimilar to those presented in Figure 5.1. The performance stressors were individual in nature and included critical moments, injury, and the outcome of the competition. The teammate stressors are related to group level events and included poor communication, teammates making mistakes, or anti-social behaviour. The external individuals' stressors were related to organisational events or individuals including the coach, officials, or the opponent. Whereas the balancing life commitments were about managing stress outside the esports environment (e.g., school commitments). Interestingly, although many of the stressors reported by the e'athletes were like those reported by traditional athletes, there were also some unique, esports specific stressors. These included technical issues, anti-social behaviour, balancing life commitments, and critical moment performance. This finding can be interpreted in two ways. First, that there are numerous similarities in the type of stressor experienced by e'athletes and traditional athletes which would indicate that interventions developed in traditional sport to deal with stress are also likely to work in esports. Also, there seem to be a small number of stressors which seem to reoccur over time. This observation is supported by a longitudinal study of elite LoL e'athletes over 87 days. In this study, a small number of reported stressors (general performance, outcome, critical moment performance, and teammate mistake) accounted for 79% of all stressors experienced (Poulus et al., 2022b). Secondly, that esports is unique in certain aspects. Technical malfunction or problems and anti-social behaviour seem related to esports and less prevalent in other sports (although technical issues would also be an issue in Formula 1 or other motor sports). How to deal with such stressors require new interventions to help e'athletes to deal with these esports specific stressors.

Finally, the study by Poulus et al. (2022a) showed that the achievement level of the e'athletes influences the type of stressors experienced. Those who were classified as elite e'athletes (those ranked in the 99%–100% percentile of their respective esports) were more likely concerned with performance issues whereas for the other e'athletes, the behaviour of their teammates was more likely to be reported as a stressor. The authors suggested that the organisational structure of esports might be related to the latter. Whereas the top players are often part of organised and stable teams most other e'athletes compete in competitions in which teammates are allocated based on game specific algorithms.

It is important to understand what kind of stressors e'athletes encounter, and further research is required to understand how the different esports genres might result in varied stressors. For example, it is essential to explore how individual esports compare to team esports in terms of the type of stressors experienced. In addition to this, the way a stressor is interpreted is also important. In particular, how e'athletes perceive control and whether a stressful event, such as participating in an important esports competition, is seen as a challenge or a threat influence subsequent coping and associated emotions.

4.2.3 Stress intensity and control

Both the intensity of the stress experienced and the perceptions of control over the stressor have been found to influence the way traditional athletes cope with stressors. In general, when a stressful event is perceived as being a threat by the e'athlete with relatively little control, they are more likely to experience unpleasant emotions (e.g., anxiety and fear) and use less adaptive coping strategies. On the other hand, when the same stressful event is appraised as a challenge and controllable the e'athlete is more likely to experience pleasant emotions (e.g., joy and excitement) and use more adaptive coping strategies. The latter is also more likely to result in better performance and increased satisfaction with the performance (see Nicholls et al., 2012).

Previous research has indicated that personality, and in particular neuroticism and mental toughness, are associated with perceptions of stress intensity and perceived control over the stressor. Athletes high in neuroticism and low in mental toughness perceive higher levels of stress intensity and report lower levels of control (Kaiseler et al., 2009, 2012). In the only study conducted on e'athletes to date, it was found that level of mental toughness did not show appraisal differences in terms of stress intensity and levels of control (Poulus et al., 2020). This was a surprising finding considering the characteristics of somebody who is deemed to be mentally tough. Hence, a mentally tough e'athlete is most likely to face situation head-on and appraise stressful encounters as a challenge to be dealt with. In addition, high in self-confidence, committed to achieve its goals, and feeling in control over its emotions and life, the e'athletes with high mental toughness is likely to perceive that they can control and deal with the stressful encounter (see Clough et al., 2002).

4.2.4 Coping with stress

Following the appraisal of an event as stressful, it is important to invoke a coping response to deal with the situation. The failure to cope with stress can have significant consequences for e'athletes. This includes decreased performance and satisfaction, health problems and injuries, withdrawal, and the inability to pursue a career in esports. Coping, in this respect, has been shown to be an explanation for differences in performance in esports. Importantly, it also provides a window for interventions.

There are numerous coping strategies which have been categorised into three higher order dimensions called problem focussed, emotion focussed, and avoidance coping (Nicholls & Polman, 2007). In general, the use of problem-focussed strategies is the most adaptive. Such strategies try to deal with the stressor there and then and include positive reframing, planning, and using instrumental support. Emotion-focussed coping includes strategies like breathing, venting, and using emotional support. These strategies are helpful in that they are likely to reduce the emotional response to the stressor (e.g., reducing anxiety or fear). However, they don't deal with the underlying problem, or, in other word, they don't solve the problem. This might manifest itself by the e'athlete making the same error time after time. Ultimately, the e'athlete must address the issue of why the error has been made which causes distress and invoke a problem-focussed coping strategy to resolve the issue. Finally, avoidance coping consists of strategies to disengage from a stressful encounter physically or mentally. For example, blocking out the pain of an injury or the verbal abuse of a teammate. Because most esports require fast decision-making and movements using avoidance coping strategies is probably not a bad approach because there is just no time to solve the problem. However, in the long term, this can be detrimental. For example, ignoring the pain of an injury can become more serious resulting in a longer time away from esports.

The earlier mentioned study by Poulus et al. (2020) examined the coping responses of e'athletes. They found that the e'athletes in their study were more likely to use acceptance and self-distraction coping strategies compared to traditional athletes. Increased use of such strategies is likely to be adaptive in esports because of the fast-paced nature of most esports as well as the online nature. In addition, the study by Poulus et al. (2020) found that e'athletes with higher levels of mental toughness used more adaptive problem-focussed coping strategies (e.g., active coping and planning) and less avoidance coping strategies (e.g., self-distraction and behavioural disengagement). This support previous research in traditional sport that examined the influence of personality traits on the stress and coping process.

A common framework which comprises most of the characteristics of personality is the Big Five model. The five traits in this model are (see Polman et al., 2010):

1 Extraversion: Energetic and open approach to your environment. Is associated with positive emotions, outgoing, and self-confident.
2 Neuroticism: Is associated with negative and unstable emotions (feeling nervous and tense), impulsive, and self-conscious.
3 Agreeableness: Being unselfish, trusting, and helpful.
4 Conscientiousness: Being purposeful (try to achieve your goals), obeying rules, planning, and being able to delay gratification to a later point in time.
5 Openness: Refers to being creative, inventive, and flexible in your thinking.

Sport research has indicated that the Big Five personality traits influence the appraisal of stressful encounters (e.g., if seen as a threat or a challenge), the intensity and control the person feels of the stressor, the selection of coping strategies and their effectiveness. In particular, neuroticism is associated with increased levels of stress, perceptions of a lack of control, selection of maladaptive coping strategies which are generally perceived as less effective (Kaiseler et al., 2012). However, more research on the role of the Big Five on esports performance and well-being is required.

More interesting for esports is the personality trait of mental toughness. In both the popular and scientific literature, being mentally tough is associated with numerous positive traits which potentially help to succeed. These include the ability to cope effectively and handle high-pressure situations and having superior mental skills. Based on the theory of hardiness, Clough et al. (2002) proposed that mental

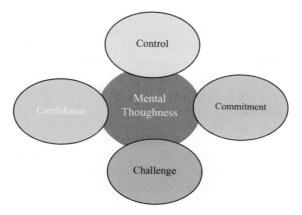

Figure 4.2 Characteristics of mental toughness according to the 4/6 Model.

toughness is associated with four key characteristics: confidence, control, commitment, and challenge (see Figure 4.2).

In this model of mental toughness, challenges are viewed as opportunities for growth, in which e'athletes persist towards their goals despite experiencing setbacks (commitment), and in which e'athletes have control over their emotions and have confidence in their abilities to succeed in their esports and/or life in general.

Poulus et al. (2020) showed that higher-ranked players in DOTA2, LoL, CS:GO, Overwatch, or Rainbow Six Siege reported higher levels of mental toughness. In additions, although mental toughness was not associated with the appraisal process, higher levels of mental toughness were associated with use of more adaptive problem-focussed coping strategies. In particular, the e'athletes with higher levels of mental toughness were more likely to use active coping, instrumental support, positive reframing, and planning and less use of avoidance coping strategies. This would indicate that more mentally tough e'athletes try to deal with the stressors head-on. Interestingly, emotion-focussed strategy of acceptance was also used more by those e'athletes higher in mental toughness. This study suggested that this might be due to the lack of control over the allocation of teammates, opponents, and characters in many esports.

4.3 Psychological skills and training

In esports it is not uncommon for e'athletes to attribute their poor performance to losing their concentration, tensing-up, or tilt situation. The solution to such issues is not spending more time behind the computer practising but to build and develop psychological skills. Considering the psychological demands in esports like dealing with stress, communicating effectively with teammates, long periods of concentration, controlling of emotions, and maintaining motivation (e.g., Murphey, 2009), it is not surprising that researchers have suggested that e'athletes would benefit from psychological skill training (PST: Cottrell et al., 2019). First, however, it is important to establish which psychological skills would benefit e'athletes. For example, it is likely that team and individual e'athletes might benefit from different psychological skills. The nature of esports might also be of influence.

A small number of studies have examined the use of psychological skills in e-athletes. In probably one of the first studies in this area, Himmelstein et al. (2017) interviewed five high level LoL players. This qualitative study resulted in two main themes: (1) strategies to achieve optimal performance and (2) obstacles preventing optimal performance. The LoL players in this study used psychological skills like imagery, goal setting, attention control, anxiety management, and motivation to improve their performance in both training and competition. In a more recent study with ten male e'athletes, eight psychological skills were identified which assisted in optimising performance across several individual and team esports. Attentional control (concentration) was perceived to be the most important psychological skill, followed by emotional control (dealing with tilt situations and frustration), activation control (dealing with pressure), communication, team cohesion (coordination, support), thought control (not overthinking), goal control (planning) and behaviour control (hold composure, temper) (Bonilla et al., 2022). Not surprisingly, communication and team cohesion were only mentioned by the team and not the individual e'athletes and all these psychological skills have been found of importance in traditional sport. Finally, Trotter et al. (2021) examined the use of psychological skills by an international sample of 1,444 e'athletes participating in either Overwatch, LoL, CS:GO, Rocket League or DOTA. When comparing their findings with a sample of swimmers, it was found that the e'athletes made more use of emotional control but significantly less of self-talk, automaticity, goal setting, imagery, relaxation, and negative thinking. A possible explanation for the lower use of psychological skills by the e'athletes in this study might be the lack of exposure. This suggestion is supported by the findings that the higher-ranked e'athletes (to 10% of their respective esport) used more self-talk, imagery, activation, and automaticity compared to the other e'athletes. Empirical evidence has shown that these four psychological skills are associated with higher performance in traditional sport. The notion that all e'athletes reported higher levels of emotional control in the study by Trotter and colleagues was attributed by the high level of anti-social behaviour in esports. Considering that this is a frequently reported stressor, the regular exposure to anti-social behaviour might have developed adaptive coping strategies in e'athletes.

Psychological skills have been shown to be effective in enhancing performance and facilitate the development of young athletes (Barker et al., 2020; Dohme et al., 2018). In addition, PST interventions have been found to enhance the effective use of these skills (see for example Rothlin et al., 2020). It is, therefore, important to consider strategies to enhance the use of these skills and identify who is best positioned to help the e'athletes to develop these psychological skills.

Despite the notion that mental aspects play an important role in achieving success in esports, few e'athletes engage in PST programs. In an ideal situation, e'athletes would work with their accredited sport psychologist to develop in a systematic way a PST program to improve their psychological skills to enhance performance and well-being by reducing mental failures (e.g., tilting and anti-social behaviour) and by increasing the ability to experience flow or get into the zone. Although several elite esports teams have accredited sport psychologists in their support staff to develop and implement PST programs, this is not the case for most e'athletes. The current esport infrastructure and organisation often fail to provide e'athletes with regular access to coaches or teachers despite the fact that psychological skills can benefit e'athletes at all levels and are not just for those who experience psychological problems. Even beginner e'athletes might greatly benefit in their development from engaging in the development of their psychological skills.

We will provide some brief information how e'athletes could start with assessing and developing their psychological skills through psychological or performance profiling (Butler & Hardy, 1992). This approach puts you as the e'athlete at the centre by creating a picture of yourself that will resonate with how you perceive yourself and will be relevant for your specific esports. The first step in this process, which can be completed individually or as a team, is to identify the key psychological skills for your esports to perform at the highest level (see Figure 4.3). Secondly, you rate between 1 and 10 where you currently think you are as an e'athlete or team. Finally, you rate the score you think is necessary to perform to the best of your ability in your esports. Having two scores for each psychological construct (your current and ideal level) provides you with a discrepancy score. In the following example, the largest discrepancy scores are for emotional control and communication. As a guide, it would probably be best to enhance your or your team's score on these two constructs to enhance performance and well-being. The next step would be to identify strategies to improve or enhance your emotional control and communication skills in these. As indicated previously, ideally you would work with an accredited sport psychologist or coach to develop and implement this. Considering this will not be possible for many e'athletes, there are numerous self-help books or information on the internet which might help to enhance your emotional control or communication skills. It is important to do this in a structured and systematic way.

Two powerful strategies to control your emotions are cognitive reappraisal and breathing. Cognitive reappraisal refers to how you can consciously change the way you interpret or handle a particular arousing event, situation, or information. Through reappraisal you can alter your emotions and importantly this can result in healthier patterns of affect, psychological well-being, and social functioning (Cutuli, 2014). For example, when facing a higher-ranked team or opponent you can appraise this as threatening and catastrophise the potential negative consequence of losing. This will create negative emotions like anxiety and fear of failure. Alternatively, you can appraise this as a challenge and put it into perspective by focussing on things you might learn from the encounter. This is likely to result in positive emotions like excitement and enjoyment.

A relatively simple and effective way to control your emotions is through your breathing. Previously, we highlighted that stress is often accompanied by shallow breathing from the chest or holding your breath rather than diaphragmatic breathing. Good breathing techniques can bring many positive effects including

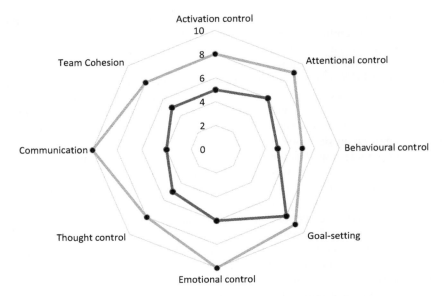

Figure 4.3 Psychological profile for LoL individual/team based on the eight psychological
skills identified by Bonilla et al. (2022). The blue line is the current state and
orange line the ideal sate.

calmness, increased energy, focus, and relaxation. Becoming aware of your breathing patterns is often the first step. Box 4.1 provides some breathing exercises which
illustrate good and bad breathing patterns (Box 4.1).

**Box 4.1   Examples of maladaptive and adaptive
breathing patterns**

Maladaptive breathing patterns

- *Chest breathing*: For this exercise you need to raise your shoulders as high
  as possible. Hold this posture for 30 seconds and observe the consequence
  of your breathing. Generally, this posture requires you to breathe from the
  upper chest rather than the abdomen. The breathing pattern will become
  shallow and quicker.
- *Holding your breath*: For this exercise try to hold your breath for 30 seconds. During this time, observe what is happening to your body. You are
  likely to feel tighter in the chest, shoulder, and neck. Repeat this two to
  three times. You might feel a bit anxious after the second or third time. This
  is what happens when you feel more anxious during competition, you are
  more likely to hold your breath.

Adaptive breathing patterns

- *Deep breathing:* For this exercise slowly inhale through your nose, first, by expanding your abdomen followed by your lungs. When breathing out first, exhale the air from the lungs before deflating your abdomen.
- *Diaphragmatic breathing:* Place one hand on your abdomen and the other on your chest. Take a deep and complete breath using your diaphragm. When you do this correctly, your hand on your abdomen should move out and in when you inhale and exhale whereas the hand on the chest stays still.
- *Sigh with exhalation:* Slowly inhale and hold your breath for 10 seconds. Holding your breath should result in building up some tension in your chest and shoulder. Now, exhale through your mouth with a slight sigh. When you do this, you should feel the tension in your chest and shoulders slip away. Repeat this three to five times. Pay attention to how you feel between the moment you have completed your exhaling and when you breathe in again. There will be a short period of calmness. Try to become aware of this and recreate this when you feel under pressure or stressed.

An important final step in performance/psychological profiling is to monitor your progress. It is important to rate yourself or your team again after a period of time to evaluate if progress has been made. Importantly, like physical skills, you must practise the psychological skills to get better at them and make them more effective. Initially, you might just practise these psychological skills away from the competitive or training environment before gradually introducing them into your training and competition regime.

4.4 Motivation

Motivational theories try to explain why e'athletes participate in certain behaviours. Why do they engage in some activities but avoid others and how much effort do they exert to achieve a certain behaviour? In sport, the athlete's motivational orientation is perceived to be important and related to 'the will to win'. As such coaches are often worried about the motivation of their athletes and try to invoke strategies to create an optimal motivational intensity. However, the problem is how coaches assess their athlete's motivation. This if often done subjectively through observation.

There are numerous theories on motivation which have been used in traditional sport. They can be categorised as either based on the individual's personality, biological (e.g., arousal) or cognitive (reasoning) aspects driving behavioural tendencies (see Box 4.2). In this chapter, we will discuss self-determination theory and growth mindset.

Box 4.2   Examples of motivational theories

Theory	Premise
Social Cognitive Theory (Bandura, 1986)	Self-efficacy: This is an individual's subjective perception or cognition to succeed in a given task at a given time. This drives choice of activity, effort, and persistence.
Sensation Seeking (Zuckerman, 1979)	Due to biological differences, some individuals need more thrills or excitement compared to others.
Theory of Need of Achievement (McClelland, 1961)	An e'athlete will avoid or engage in competitions because of the motive to succeed (desire to excel) or avoid failure.
Self-Motivation (Dishman & Ickes, 1981)	The tendency to continue in a behaviour unrelated of situational incentives.
Goal Setting (e.g., Lock et al., 1981)	(Self) Motivational strategy to improve performance through directing attention, encouraging enhanced intensity and continuance. Achieving the goal will improve motivation, self-efficacy, satisfaction, and future performance.

4.4.1 Self-determination theory

Self-determination theory (e.g., Deci & Ryan, 1985, 2000) is a well-recognised theory which has been examined extensively in sport to understand behaviours and well-being. The main premise is that motivation is determined by an individual's feelings of autonomy (choice and willingness to one's behaviour), competence (experience of mastery and being effective in one's behaviour) and relatedness (feel connected and belongingness with others). This, in turn, is associated with three forms of motivation: intrinsic, extrinsic, and a-motivation, and their regulatory styles (see Figure 4.4).

The best form of motivation is intrinsic. When e'athletes are intrinsically motivated to play esports they do this because they receive a sense of pleasure and satisfaction whilst putting in significant effort and dedication to improve their skills. Although integrated regulation is a form of extrinsic motivation, this is still a desirable form of motivation. The e'athlete would participate in esports because they have identified themselves with the activity. In addition, it would satisfy their psychological needs of autonomy, competence, and relatedness. Consequently, effort and engagement will be high. Identified regulation refers to e'athletes engaging in esports because it will help them to achieve their personal goals such as learning new skills. Playing esports is a means to an end. Introjected regulation refers to the e'athlete feeling compelled to do so to avoid external disapproval or externally referenced approval.

External regulation refers to the e'athlete being motivated to taking part in esports for external rewards (money, points), whilst avoiding punishment. Finally, a-motivated means that somebody is not interested in the esports, it has no personal meaning (see Hagger & Chatzisarantis, 2007).

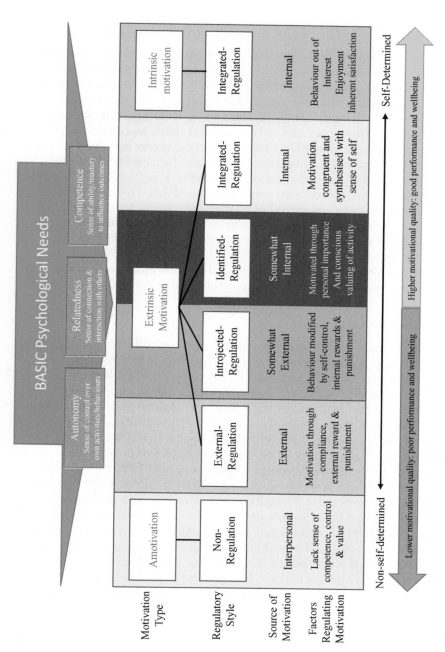

Figure 4.4 Adapted summary of the self-determination theory.

Whereas there are numerous factors which can undermine an e'athletes intrinsic motivation there are strategies coaches could apply to enhance feelings of autonomy, competence, and relatedness and as such intrinsic motivation. These include:

1 Autonomy: Provide choice, perceptions of control and personal responsibility. This could be achieved by asking e'athletes to assist in organising practice sessions, the dress code or development of tactical strategies. The coach needs to be sure that e'athletes can make independent decisions so that they feel ownership over their own development. By the same token, avoid threats or impose goals.
2 Competence: Practice sessions and competitions should be challenging but provide successful experience. If e'athletes experience success, they are likely to feel more competent and want to continue practicing Coaches should also provide positive verbal or non-verbal performance feedback and acknowledgement of each e'athlete importance to the team's success and goal. This could be achieved by varying the order and context of practice drills. E'athletes need the opportunity to explore through, for example, playing in different positions in the team.
3 Relatedness: Coaches should provide a respectful, safe, and inclusive environment trying to avoid criticism and cliques. Also, coaches should develop meaningful relationships with their e'athletes and facilitate this among the e'athletes. The latter could be achieved through (unsupervised) training or social activities.

4.4.2 Growth mindset

Mindsets generally refer to our implicit beliefs about ourselves. They commonly refer to traits (e.g., your academic performance) which some people believe are fixed whilst others think these can be changed through experiences and learning. An individual with a growth mindset, in this respect, would attribute their academic performance to the magnitude of practice and work exerted whereas a fixed mindset would suggest that this is predetermined (Dweck et al., 1995). A fixed and growth mindset can be viewed as opposites; however, research has shown that this can be changed and developed (Costa & Faria, 2018). The concept of a growth mindset has important implications in terms of learning and goal setting, and ultimately performance.

An e'athlete with a growth mindset is more likely to tackle a challenging situation by taking actions and making efforts to improve their skills or abilities to master the task. They set mastery goals and if they fail to achieve their goals, they will attribute it to insufficient effort or poor strategies. An e'athlete with a fixed mindset, on the other hand, will likely set performance goals which are related to demonstrating competence and outperforming opponents. The problem arises when they can't achieve difficult challenges because this attributed to their belief that their skills and abilities are predetermined. This can result in learned helplessness: basically, the e'athlete would give up because they think they are not good enough (low perceptions of self-efficacy beliefs) despite that there are solutions to the problem at hand (e.g., Ames, 1992; Dweck & Leggett, 1988). Intervention studies, mainly in academic settings, have shown that this can result in greater engagement, interest, and higher performance, in particular, in those students who are performing poorly (e.g., Hecht et al., 2021). Interestingly, such interventions can be relatively short. In a study by Yeager et al. (2019), a one-hour intervention proved effective in increasing mathematical performance among underperforming students.

The growth mindset concept appears to be an important motivational model which will influence whether e'athletes will try harder or give-up in developing their skills. Coaches could easily assess their players' growth mindset (https://sparqtools.org/mobility-measure/growth-mindset-scale/) and help their e'athletes to set mastery rather than performance goals and applaud improvements rather than outcomes. Mastery goals enhance effort and persistence and can create new attitudes (e.g., I can't do this yet…). In this view, failure is seen as a chance to learn and develop as an e'athlete and see challenges as a way to improve. It is easy to see how a growth mindset relates to the concept of competence in Self-Determination Theory. In addition, autonomy and perceptions of control are important for the development of a growth mindset.

References

Ames, C. (1992). Classrooms: Goals, structures, and student motivation. *Journal of Education Psychology, 84*, 261–271.

Bandura, A. (1986). *Social foundations of thought and action: A social cognitive theory.* Englewood Cliffs, NJ: Prentice-Hall.

Barker, J. B., Slater, M. J., Pugh, G., Mellalieu, S. D., McCarty, P. J., Jones, M. V., & Moran, A. (2020). The effectiveness of psychological skill training and behavioural interventions in sport using single-case designs: A meta regression analysis of the peer-reviewed studies. *Psychology of Sport & Exercise, 51*, 101746.

Bonilla, I., Chamarro, A., & Ventura, C. (2022). Psychological skills in esports: Qualitative study of individual and team players. *Revista de Psicologia, 40*(1), 35–41.

Butler, R. J., & Hardy, L. (1992). The performance profile: Theory and application. *The Sport Psychologist, 6*, 253–264.

Clough, P. J., Earle, K., & Sewell, D. (2002). Mental toughness: The concept and its measurement. In I. Cockrill (Ed.), *Solution in sport psychology* (pp. 32–43). London: Thompson.

Costa, A., & Faria, L. (2018). Implicit theories of intelligence and academic achievement: A meta-analytic review. *Frontiers in Psychology, 9*, 829.

Cottrell, C., McMillen, N., & Harris, B. S. (2019). Sport psychology in a virtual world: Considerations for practitioners working in esports. *Journal of Sport Psychology in Action, 10*(2), 73–81.

Cutuli, D. (2014). Cognitive reappraisal and expressive suppression strategies role in the emotion regulation: An overview on their modulatory effects and neural correlates. *Frontiers in Systems Neuroscience, 8*, 175.

Deci, E., & Ryan, R. M. (1985). *Intrinsic motivation and self-determination in human behavior.* New York: Kluwer Academic/Plenum Publishers.

Deci, E., & Ryan, R. M. (2000). The 'what' and 'why' of goal pursuits: Human needs and self-determination behaviour. *Psychological Inquiry, 11*, 227–268.

Dishman, R. K., & Ickes, W. (1981). Self-motivation and adherence to therapeutic exercise. *Journal of Behavioural Medicine, 4*, 421–438.

Dohme, L.-C., Piggott, D., Backhouse, S., & Morgan, G. (2018). Psychological skills and characteristics facilitative of youth athletes' development: A systematic review. *The Sport Psychologist, 33*(4), 261–275.

Dweck, C. S., Chiu, C.-Y., & Hong, Y.-Y. (1995). Implicit theories and their role in judgements and reactions: A word from two perspectives. *Psychological Inquiry, 4*, 267–285.

Dweck, C. S., & Leggett, E. L. (1988). A social-cognitive approach to motivation and personality. *Psychological Review, 95*(2), 256–273.

Hagger, M. S., & Chatzisarantis, N. L. D. (2007). *Intrinsic motivation and self-determination in exercise and sport.* Champaign, IL: Human Kinetics.

Hecht, C. A., Yeager, D. S., Dweck, C. S., & Murphy, M. C. (2021). Beliefs, affordances, and adolescent development: Lessons from a decade of growth mindset interventions. *Advances in Child Development and Behaviour, 61*, 169–197.

Himmelstein, D., Liu, Y., & Shapiro, J. L. (2017). An exploration of mental skills among competitive league of legend players. *International Journal of Gaming and Computer-Mediated Simulations, 9*(2), 1–21.

Kaiseler, M., Polman, R. C. J., & Nicholls, A. R. (2009). Mental toughness, stress, stress appraisal, coping and coping effectiveness in sport. *Personality and Individual Differences, 47*, 728–733.

Kaiseler, M., Polman, R. C. J., & Nicholls, A. R. (2012). Indirect and direct effects of the Big Five Personality dimensions on appraisal, coping and coping effectiveness in sport. *European Journal of Sport and Exercise Science, 12*(1), 62–72.

Lock, E. A., Shaw, K. N., Saari, L. M., & Latham, G. P. (1981). Goal setting and task performance: 1969–1980. *Psychological Bulletin, 90*, 125–152.

Madden, D., & Harteveld, C. (2021). Constant pressure of having to perform: Exploring player health concerns in esports. In *CHI Conference on Human Factors in Computing Systems*, May 8–13, Yokohama, Japan.

McClelland, D. C. (1961). The achieving society. *History and Theory, 3*(3), 371–381.

Murphey, S. (2009). Video games, competition and exercise: A new opportunity for sport psychologists? *The Sport Psychologist, 23*(4), 487–503.

Nicholls, A. R., & Polman, R. C. J. (2007). Coping in sport: A systematic review. *Journal of Sports Sciences, 25*(1), 11–31.

Nicholls, A. R., Polman, R. C. J., & Levy, A. R. (2012). A path analysis of stress appraisal, emotions, coping and performance satisfaction among athletes. *Psychology of Sport and Exercise, 13*, 263–270.

Polman, R. C. J., Clough, P. J., & Levy, A. R. (2010). Chapter 8: Personality and coping in sport: The big five and mental toughness (pp. 141–157). In A. R. Nicholls (Ed.), *Coping in sport: Theory, methods, and related constructs* (pp. 79–93). New York: Nova Science Publishers.

Poulus, D., Coulter, T., Trotter, M., & Polman, R. (2022a). Perceived stressors experienced by competitive esports athletes. *International Journal of Esports, 1*(1), 1–14.

Poulus, D. R., Coulter, T. J., Trotter, M. G., & Polman, R. (2022b). Longitudinal analysis of stressors, stress, coping and coping effectiveness in elite esports athletes. *Psychology of Sport & Exercise, 60*, 102093.

Poulus, D. R., Coulter, T. J., Trotter, M. G., & Polman, R. (2020). Stress and coping in esports and the influence of mental toughness. *Frontiers in Psychology, 11*, 628.

Rothlin, P., Horvath, S., Trosch, S., Holtforth, M. G., & Birrer, D. (2020). Differential and shared effects of psychological skills training and mindfulness training on performance relevant psychological factors in sprot: A randomized controlled trial. *BMC Psychology, 8*, 80.

Trotter, M. G., Coulter, T. J., Davis, P. A., Poulus, D. R., & Polman, R. (2021). Social support, self-regulation, and psychological skill use in e-athletes. *Frontiers in Psychology, 12*, 722030.

Yeager, D. S., Hanselman, P., Walton, G. M., Murray, J. S., Crosnoe, R., Muller, C., et al. (2019). A national experiment reveals where a growth mindset improves achievement. *Nature, 573*, 364–369.

Zuckerman, M. A. (1979). Sensation seeking and risk taking. In C. E. Izard (Ed.), *Emotions in personality and psychopathology* (pp. 161–179). London: Springer.

5 Nutrition, supplementation, and regulation

Craig McNulty

5.1 Introduction

Accurately guiding an e'athlete's nutrition, for health and performance, is best achieved with at least a fundamental understanding of human metabolism, biochemistry, food science, and nutrition programming. This chapter first introduces the reader to the basics of human metabolism – from ingestion of food to the biochemical transfer of energy within a cell – before focussing on the effects of nutrition on cognitive function, muscular health, cardiovascular health, and mental well-being as it relates to e'athletes' health and performance. The science and measurement of body composition, energy expenditure, and nutritional programming are then discussed. Finally, this chapter addresses nutritional trends in esports, dietary maintenance and nutrition scheduling, medications and their interactions with metabolism, ergogenic aids, and banned substances. By the end of the chapter, the reader will have a fundamental understanding of human nutrition as it applies to esports, including the capability to advise e'athletes and achieve essential nutritional programming.

5.2 Overview of human biochemistry and metabolism

Human biochemistry and metabolism are exceedingly complex, not just in terms of these processes within the body during normal day-to-day activity but also in terms of the immediate and long-term effects of diet, exercise, medications, disease, injury, emotional and physical stress, and even external factors such as climate and altitude. Human biochemistry remains one of the most taught topics across medical and health science degrees. It is biochemistry which forms the foundation of all biological processes within the human body and can help develop a greater understanding of the impact of food choices, nutritional needs, and caloric requirements for health and performance.

The primary constituents of ingested food are proteins (PRO), carbohydrates (CHO), and fats (FAT), referred to as macronutrients. Along with macronutrients, food contains a vast array of micronutrients in the form of vitamins (such as vitamins B and C, or water-soluble vitamins; and vitamins A, D, E, K, or fat-soluble vitamins), minerals (such as calcium, magnesium, and potassium), trace minerals

DOI: 10.4324/9781003322382-5

(such as iron, zinc, and fluoride), and finally water. Macronutrients primarily drive biological functions which require energy transfer, including muscular contraction and nerve cell action potential propagation, as well as intra/extracellular signalling, DNA resynthesis, and cellular repair and reproduction (Champe et al., 2005). Vitamins, minerals, and trace minerals support an array of functions in the body such as immunity, blood clotting, promotion of bone growth, oxygen transport, hormonal regulation, and digestive system health (Mann & Truswell, 2012). Finally, water assists in body temperature regulation, nutrient transport and metabolic by-product removal, digestion, and many other functions (Jéquier & Constant, 2010).

Following ingestion of food, macronutrients such as PRO, CHO, and FAT are mechanically and chemically digested into their base constituents of amino acids, glucose, and fatty acids, respectively. Each of these organic subunits can follow a specific metabolic (or energy) pathway to assist in replenishing adenosine triphosphate (ATP). ATP is an organic compound consisting of an adenine base, ribose sugar, and three phosphate groups. The chemical energy stored within the bonds of the phosphate groups of ATP is released (ATP hydrolysis) at specific sites within a cell, and are responsible for muscle contraction (by binding and releasing small contractile filaments and myosin heads within muscle) and nerve cell propagation (by activation – and by extension, inhibition – of sodium and potassium pathways [gates] along nerve cell walls). Following the transfer of energy from the phosphate bonds of ATP, the phosphate group is split from the ATP molecule, forming two molecules: adenosine diphosphate (ADP) and an inorganic phosphate. When we talk about replenishing ATP (ATP resynthesis), we essentially mean the biochemical process of reforming these bonds between the free phosphate group and ADP. ATP resynthesis must keep up with ATP demand, which is primarily dictated by energy output. The higher the energy output (say, during a moderate or high-intensity run), the higher the rate of ATP resynthesis. The balancing of energy demand and ATP resynthesis assists in maintaining homeostasis – the condition of optimal biological functioning. Of course, when ATP resynthesis can no longer match ATP demand, we begin to experience fatigue (discussed in Chapter 3), until ultimately, we cease activity to begin recovery to replenish ATP and remove excess by-products of metabolism. The process of ATP resynthesis occurs via three interrelated biochemical pathways: (1) the phosphagen (ATP-PCr) system, (2) glycolysis, and (3) oxidative metabolism. All three systems contribute to ATP resynthesis at any time, however, the intensity of an activity (such as walking, running, or sprinting) will dictate the relative contribution of these systems to ATP resynthesis (Figure 5.1). CHO and FAT (and to a far less extent, PRO) substrates are the key drivers of glycolysis and oxidative metabolism. The relative ATP turnover rates of these energy pathways are summarised in Figure 5.2. While these energy pathways, and the nutrients that fuel them, work to maintain homeostasis above the rest by balancing ATP resynthesis with demand, it must be remembered that these processes don't immediately resolve upon ceasing activity. Rather, there is a post-exercise increased energy demand above rest that continues for some time after stopping an activity or exercise. This period is referred to as metabolic recovery, which occurs alongside tissue repair following exercise (Gaesser & Brooks, 1984).

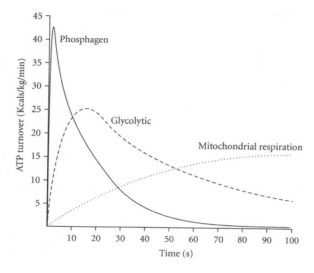

Figure 5.1 Interaction between exercise intensity (indicative of the length of time to fatigue) and ATP turnover (Baker et al., 2010).

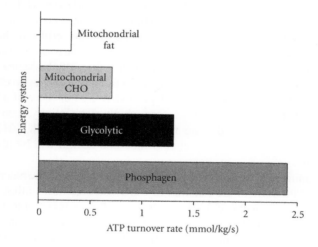

Figure 5.2 Maximal rates of ATP turnover for the independent energy pathways in skeletal muscle (Baker et al., 2010).

Excess post-exercise oxygen consumption (EPOC) is a measurably higher oxygen uptake (cellular oxygen metabolism during ATP resynthesis within the cell mitochondria), above relative rest values, that occurs for minutes to hours following the cessation of physical activity or exercise (LaForgia et al., 2006). The increased oxygen-dependence post-exercise is due to the continued need to replenish ATP following exercise. Depending on the intensity of the activity, individuals will experience the physical effects of EPOC as an increase in ventilation (breathing frequency and volume of inspiration and expiration), increased heart rate, and increased skin temperature (and perhaps sweating) above rest. During EPOC, FAT is the primary substrate that continues to be metabolised during recovery, and at very high intensity exercise, CHO metabolism will have increased contribution to recovery immediately post-exercise. While this period of EPOC is physically noticeable during the immediate phases of recovery, it has been shown to continue for significantly longer periods (exercise intensity and duration dependent) after physical effects are no longer noticeable (Bahr et al., 1987; LaForgia et al., 1997; Phelain et al., 1997; Quinn et al., 1994). There have been a multitude of experimental studies since the early 1900s investigating the effect of exercise intensity, duration, mode, and training types on EPOC (Børsheim & Bahr, 2003), with results indicating the recovery EPOC period lasting from minutes (Sedlock, 1991; Smith & McNaughton, 1993) up to hours and even days (Børsheim et al., 1994; Hermansen et al., 1984). During this period of heightened oxygen demand, there will be an increase in FAT and CHO metabolism, which will diminish over time until the body returns to a rested homeostatic state.

Macronutrients which are not being used for ATP resynthesis, nor excreted as waste, are stored within the body. Glycogen (a stored form of CHO made of many connected glucose molecules) stores within the muscle and liver, while excess glucose unable to be stored as glycogen (due to biological limits) will convert to FAT through a process called lipogenesis. FAT is stored as triglycerides within adipose tissue, which is a connective tissue found under the skin (subcutaneous) and around the internal organs (visceral) of the body. To maintain healthy biological function, the body requires a minimal level of storage of FAT and CHO (Dragoo et al., 2021; Ørtenblad et al., 2013). The body may adapt to store less or more of a macronutrient based on factors such as daily EE through physical activity, environmental factors, and as an outcome of disease and health (Thompson et al., 2012). Excess storage, and its effects on the body composition and health, will be discussed in the next section.

At the beginning of this section of the chapter, we introduced the macronutrients CHO, FAT, and PRO. With the function of CHO and FAT now outlined in terms of ATP resynthesis to meet energy demands, we will now turn to PRO synthesis. Unlike CHO and FAT, PRO's primary contribution to biosynthesis isn't related to energy demands of activity and living, rather the repair of damaged or excreted cellular proteins (Gropper & Smith, 2013). PRO resynthesis contributes to enzyme (catalysts for molecular change) production, hormone production, and cellular structural repair. Above normal biological turnover, PRO significantly contributes to cellular repair following acute exercise. Atherton and Smith (2012) attributed the PRO availability through food due to daily intake as the primary contributor of muscle repair following acute exercise (this is also a reason why athletes consume protein shakes following a workout). Adult nutritional needs for health and esports performance, as they relate the PRO, CHO, and FAT, will be discussed in the next section.

5.3 Adult nutrition, health, and behaviour change

Individual adult nutritional needs are defined by several biological and environmental factors including mass, sex, genetics, regionality, daily EE, and may be influenced by personal factors such as food aversion, cultural and religious expectations, and food availability. The following guidelines of adult nutrition are based on the World Health Organization (WHO, 2020) Healthy Diet guidelines. However, individual factors should be considered when developing a nutritional plan. For athletes, consultation should occur during nutritional programming and maintain an athlete-centred approach in terms of health-based decision-making.

The WHO (2020) recommends the following for a healthy adult diet (based on a daily 2,000 calorie per day requirement):

- At least 400 g of fruit and vegetables, including legumes, nuts, and whole grains (excluding potatoes and starchy roots)
- Less than 10% of daily EE as free sugars (preferably less than 5%), including those added to foods and drinks and those naturally present in fruit juices, syrups, and honey
- Less than 30% of total energy intake from fats, and preferably unsaturated fats, such as those found in fish, avocado, nuts, and olive oil. Saturated fats, such as those in fatty meats, butter, and cheese, should be limited. Trans-fats, such as those found in fried foods and pre-packaged industrially-produced foods should be avoided altogether.

These recommendations have been shown to reduce the risk of lifestyle disease such as cardiovascular disease and type 2 diabetes. In terms of daily PRO intake, the American College of Sports Medicine (ACSM, 2011) recommends that individuals consume 0.8 g of PRO per kg of body weight per day. Finally, the recommendation for daily water intake is 2.2 L and 2.9 L for a 58 kg female and 70 kg male, respectively. Although, these water intake recommendations will greatly vary depending on daily physical activity and ambient temperature, with daily intake of up to 4.5 L for both males and females as necessary (Howard & Bartram 2003; WHO, 2005).

In Chapter 3, we discussed the importance of exercise induced adaptations to cognitive function, muscular health, cardiovascular efficiency, and mental well-being. We will now address these key outcomes of esports performance and health in terms of nutrition. Remember that optimal cognitive functioning for an e'athlete often relates to the domains of memory, strategic thinking, attention, task-switching, and information processing. A review conducted by Ribeiro and colleagues (2021) examined specifically esports nutrition and identified several findings relating to nutrition and cognitive indicators of performance.

While the average age of all gamers is around 35 years (Jovanovic, 2022), the mean age of professional esports players is much younger with the top 100 esports players averaging 25.7 years (Mamerow, 2022). In 2017, the average age of a Major League Baseball player was 29.2 years, and 26.6 years was the average age of a player in the National Football League (ESPN, 2017). However, CS:GO player ages averaged at 23.4 years, while LoL players were on average 21.2 years of age (ESPN, 2017). Esports players often turn professionals in their early 20s and even mid-late adolescent years. Jadon Ashman, for example, turned a professional in Fortnite at the age of 16 (Mamerow, 2022). This is particularly important when we consider e'athlete nutrition, as we also need to consider not only the effects of nutrition on cognitive outcomes, but also the cognitive effects of nutrition on a developing brain. A review by Naveed and colleagues (2020) linked poor diet quality with impairments in cognitive functioning in children and adolescents, with some mechanisms of diet having a direct or synergistic effect on the brain. Furthermore, a 'Western' diet with high intakes of saturated fats, refined sugars and cereal, sodium, and alcohol is associated with diminished cognitive performance in adolescents and adults (Nyaradi et al., 2014; Ribeiro et al., 2021). Ribeiro (2021) further validated the findings that poor diet may have negative effects in terms of cognition and memory during the brain's developmental phase from birth to approximately 25 years of age (Arain et al., 2013). As well, a high sugar and fat diet is linked to decreases in cognitive function and may have negative influence on hippocampal function which is involved in memorisation and learning (Ribeiro et al., 2021). A diet composed mainly of whole grains, legumes, vegetables, fruit, and fish may decrease risk of cognitive impairments (Ribeiro et al., 2021).

Of course, there are considerations that extend further than simply educating e'athletes on optimal diet for health and performance. Three key items for consideration are:

1 The e'athletes' receptiveness to dietary change
2 Nutrition education, alongside implementation
3 The timeframe for nutritional programming

As with any lifestyle-related changes (such as exercise, mental well-being practice, smoking cessation, and dietary changes), it is important to identify the e'athlete's readiness for change. This will inform the rapidity and intensity of dietary change implementation. The transtheoretical model of behaviour change (Prochaska & Velicer, 1997) is an integrative behaviour therapy model that assesses an individual's readiness for behaviour change originally devised for use in psychotherapy. It is now broadly used within the fields of psychology and clinical health to assist practitioners in best practice for implementing lifestyle and behaviour changes, such as dietary programming. The model aims to place an individual within one of five distinct categories: *precontemplation, contemplation, preparation, action, maintenance,* and *relapse.* The categories are summarised in Table 5.1. It is suggested that esports practitioners familiarise themselves with this model to assist in nutritional interventions.

Health care strategies are evolving to place more emphasis on patient education, and to maintain a patient-centred approach to health care interventions (Silverman et al., 2013). This approach has improved patient health outcomes and perceptions. The same approach should be taken with e'athletes, as nutritional plans are

Table 5.1 Transtheoretical Model of Behaviour Change Stages, Athlete Characteristics, and Counselling Strategies

Stage	Athlete Characteristics	Counselling Strategies
Precontemplation	No intention to change, low awareness	Increasing awareness of importance, begin dialogue
Contemplation	Intention to change, ambivalence, low self-confidence for change	Highlight benefits, address ambivalence, build self-confidence
Preparation	Intending to take action, making small changes, may have previously attempted change	Assist with planning, provide resources and further education
Action	Recently changed behaviour, in need of support, high risk of relapse	Promote social support, provide encouragement, develop relapse mitigation strategies
Maintenance	Undergone change for a long period (~6 months or more), high self-confidence	Refine and add variety to programming, continued support to prepare/avoid relapse
Relapse	Can occur at the action or maintenance stage, likelihood diminishes the longer the athlete has practised positive change	Identify reason for relapse, develop strategies with athlete to raise awareness of triggers to avoid future relapse

implemented. The esports practitioner should outline the importance and necessity of nutritional intervention strategies in terms of improvements in performance and health. A regular e'athlete check-in and follow-up, both in terms of objective outcomes (for example, healthy weight maintenance, cognitive skills, glucose regulation) and subjective outcomes (such as mood, sleep, and attitudes towards nutrition), will assist the practitioner in maintaining the e'athlete program adherence or altering the program as necessary to improve adherence and measurable outcomes.

Finally, drawing on both previous key items, the practitioner should develop a nutritional intervention timeline with the e'athlete's needs and readiness for change in mind. As with many health interventions, adherence is often benefitted by making small alterations to current lifestyle practices over a longer period. Substantial changes to current player lifestyle over a short period can often result in attrition. Once the practitioner has identified the degree of dietary change necessary for improvement of health and esports performance, conversations should be had with the e'athlete around the best method for introducing these changes.

5.3.1 Nutrition scheduling

An important factor for nutrition programming is nutrient timing. Kerksick and colleagues (2017) published a position stand on sports nutrient timing, specifically relating to PRO and CHO for performance and recovery. Although the energy expenditure for esports is likely much less than most sports, due to the lower physical requirement, the science of nutrient timing is still applicable. As well, there is preliminary research supporting nutrient timing in esports for cognitive performance

(Ribeiro, et al., 2021; Turner, 2023). From this research, several key points have been identified:

- Meal timing (that is, the period of time before or after an activity that a meal is consumed) has a perceived effect on the e'athletes performance, with e'athletes reporting the consumption of meals close to a game start time may elicit feelings of tiredness, although the composition of these meals is likely to have more of a substantial impact on performance (Ribeiro et al., 2021; Turner, 2023).
- E'athletes reported pre-game meals that are high-fat, 'sugary', or large portion sizes had a detrimental effect on performance (Turner, 2023). However, it was reported that pre-game meals that were low-fat, low-sugar, or even moderate fasting had a perceived positive effect on performance (Turner, 2023).
- Habitual dietary behaviour such as increasing fruit and vegetables, increasing high-quality carbohydrates, reducing portion sizes, and regular meal patterns were reported as improving esports performance. While chronic dehydration and habitual diets rich in fast food and high-fat/high-sugar foods were reported as detrimental to esports performance (Turner, 2023).
- Meal skipping (especially, breakfast) correlates with inferior attention, executive function, and memory in young adults (Ackuaku-Dogbe, 2014; Adolphus et al., 2016). As well, hunger and thirst at any stage in the day prior and during esports play were reported as distractions that may impact performance (Turner, 2023).

Having gained a general understanding of biochemical factors of nutrition, adult nutrition and behaviour, and nutrient scheduling, we can now begin to understand the development of nutrition planning for e'athletes. The following section will discuss body compositional measures and energy expenditure, which will allow us to develop an evidence-based daily nutrition plan.

5.4 Understanding body composition, and defining daily energy expenditure

Previously, we discussed an overview of biochemical aspects of PRO, CHO, and FATs in metabolism. It was noted that the varying substrates of these macronutrients are the key drivers of metabolism, and therefore chemical energy production within the cells. The relative necessity of each of these macronutrients is defined by several factors, including body composition, sex, basal metabolic rate (BMR) and resting metabolic rate (RMR), physical activity (above RMR), and the thermic effect of food. As well, considerations need to be made for the specific substrates of macronutrients. PRO can be broken down into 20 distinct amino acids, some of which are essential (those which cannot be produced by the body and therefore must be consumed through food) and some non-essential (can be produced within the body). Similarly, there are several unique dietary fatty acids (substrates of FAT) which are categorised as *saturated, monounsaturated,* and *polyunsaturated.* Finally, CHO substrates include monosaccharides (glucose, fructose, and galactose), disaccharides (lactose, sucrose, maltose, and trehalose), as well as long-chain (or complex carbohydrates) oligosaccharides and polysaccharides (such as starch and glycogen).

Similar to exercise programming for an e'athlete, dietary programming is best achieved through individual prescription based on the e'athlete's needs. Understanding the functions of macronutrient substrates, and the nutrient composition of foods, as well as the health and energy expenditure needs of an e'athlete, is necessary for best dietary advice for health and performance. Indirectly, body compositional measures can be used to guide an individual nutrition prescription. Assessing body composition can be achieved through a wide variety of measures, with some requiring minimal training and equipment (such as body mass indexing, waist circumference, and skinfold assessment), while others requiring specialised technicians and expensive equipment (dual X-ray absorptiometry and under water weighing). It is important that a practitioner considers the validity of a measurement, as well as the expertise necessary, and the cost of the equipment when considering different body compositional measures. Using multiple assessments in conjunction with one another can improve the accuracy of the estimates (in fact, all body compositional assessments are estimates and indirect measures). Waist circumference is a simple measurement requiring only a fabric tape measure, which has shown to be valid compared to computer tomographic measurement.

With the results of these simple measurements, the esports practitioner or an e'athlete will have a preliminary understanding of the current body composition and health, and can estimate their BMR, to begin to understand their baseline energy intake requirements. BMR is defined as the metabolic rate of an individual at rest in a room temperature environment, and during a postabsorptive state (that is, fasted for 8–12 hours) (Hulbert & Else, 2004), and is therefore best measured immediately upon waking. It is the rate at which the body expends energy for life-sustaining biological processes such as heartbeat, respiration, renal function, and blood circulation (Gropper & Smith, 2013), and contributes to approximately 70% of total daily EE in young to middle-aged adults, and gradually declines in older age (Pontzer et al., 2021). BMR values are presented in units of kilocalories (kcal). Measurement of BMR requires expired gas analysis by indirect calorimetry. Many physiology laboratories, and some sports institutes have these devices available, however smaller-scale sports institutes and clubs are unlikely to have access to indirect calorimetry. Because of this, equations to estimate BMR, as well as RMR and energy expenditure (EE) have been defined. Of course, with any estimate comes a degree of error, and the following examples of BMR estimates have limitations that need to be considered when adopting this process.

The below are the commonly used Harris-Benedict (Harris & Benedict, 1919) predictive equations for estimating adult BMR:

BMR (kcal) for Men = 66.47 + (13.75 * weight [kg])
+ (5.003 * height [cm]) − (6.755 * age [years])
BMR (kcal) for Women = 655.1 + (9.563 * weight [kg])
+ (1.85 * height [cm]) − (4.676 * age [years])

(Harris & Benedict, 1919)

It should be noted that these equations have inherent error due to their predictive nature, which becomes especially apparent when applied to obese individuals, as well as different ethnicities (Bendavid et al., 2021; Douglas et al., 2007). The variations in estimate accuracy were identified in a review by Bendavid et al., 2021. Nonetheless, the equations are simple to apply (only requiring a height and a mass measurement) and create a beginning point for understanding the energy expenditure of an e'athlete, and therefore nutritional needs.

Once an e'athlete's BMR has been estimated, it is time to calculate their energy expenditure above their basal rate. This is determined by several factors previously mentioned, with physical activity being the next biggest contributor to daily EE. While BMR accounts for approximately 50%–70% of total daily EE (Ravussin & Bogardus, 1992), physical activity can account for approximately 10%–40% (Gropper & Smith, 2013). Naturally, this value is heavily dependent on how physically active an individual is throughout the day, with sedentary individuals having the lowest relative expenditure (Bernstein et al., 1999). There are several methods for measuring daily physical activity, with varying degrees of costs and expertise required (Ndahimana & Kim, 2017). Doubly-labelled water and direct or indirect calorimetry are considered the gold standard measures of EE, however, the cost of the hardware and expertise for these measures often leaves them inaccessible for those not employed within a research university, physiology laboratory, or a well-funded sporting institute. However, there are several cost-effective methods of collecting daily activity data, such as heart rate monitors, pedometry, or self-report and physical activity diaries. Heart rate devices and pedometers are relatively low-cost tools for collecting objective movement and exercise data. Many modern sports and smart watches include heart rate measurement and step counting hardware and software. These devices often estimate daily EE based on these variables, and report this through the device's interface. Alternatively, e'athletes can complete daily or weekly activity surveys, or maintain physical activity diaries, where the e'athlete will report on duration, frequency, and intensity of day-to-day activities above rest. These values can then be converted to a metabolic equivalent of the task (MET), which is a ratio of EE relative to the individual's mass, based on an assumed oxygen uptake where 1 MET = 3.5 mL O_2.kg.min^{-1}, or – as it will be expressed herein – defined as 1 kcal.kg.hr. Using MET equivalents of common physical activity or exercise, as outlined in Table 5.2, an e'athlete or coach may calculate daily MET minutes to be used as a predictor of daily workload (Ainsworth et al., 2000; Haskell et al., 2007).

With an understanding of METs related to exercise and daily activities, alongside the predictive equations for men and women, we can now estimate daily energy expenditure. The following example illustrates the case of a female 22-year-old competitive e'athlete, with a mass of 58 kg and a height of 164 cm. The reported daily activities (example displayed in Table 5.3) could be identified through a retrospective self-report, or an activity diary maintained by the e'athlete. It is advised that coaches have the e'athlete complete an activity diary across several days, including weekdays and weekends, due to routine changes (and potential EE of activity changes) throughout a week.

Table 5.2 MET Guidelines for Common Sports and Daily Activities

Light < 3.0 METs	*Moderate 3.0 – 6.0 METs*	*Vigorous > 6.0 METs*
Walking (slow) = 2.0	Walking (5 km/h) = 3.3	Brisk walk (7.2 km/h) = 6.3
Sitting and light work (office computer work) = 1.5	Walking (6.5 km/h) = 5.0	Jogging (8 km/h) = 8.0
Standing and light work (ironing, preparing food) = 2.0–2.5	Upright housework (sweeping, vacuuming) = 3.0–3.5	Running (11.3 km/h) = 11.5
Arts & craft = 1.5	Mowing lawn = 5.5	Basketball game = 8.0
Playing a musical instrument = 2.0–2.5	Cycling (flat surface, 16–19 km/h) = 6.0	Cycling (flat surface, 22.5–26 km/h) = 10.0
	Golf (no cart) = 4.3	Football (soccer) = 10.0
	Swimming (leisure) = 6.0	Tennis = 8.0

Adapted from Ainsworth et al. (2000), Haskell et al. (2007).

Table 5.3 A Simulated Activity Diary for an E'athlete, Including MET Costs of Activities

Daily Activity	*Time (hr)*	*MET Cost*	*Time × MET*
Sleeping	8	1	8
Eating	1	1.5	1.5
Practice (esports)	6	2.0	12
Study (at home office)	4	1.5	6
Walking dog	0.5	3.5	1.75
Run (11 km/hr)	0.5	11	5.5
Cooking	1	2	2
Watching TV	3	1.5	4.5
	24		**41.25**

Initially, we will calculate the BMR of our e'athlete:

BMR = 655.1 + (9.563 * 58) + (1.85 * 164) − (4.676 * 22)
BMR = 1,410 kcal

We now need to estimate the energy cost of the e'athlete's daily activity in METs, which can then be converted to kcal. Table 5.3 is our e'athlete's activity diary of the previous 24 hours.

As seen in the table, our e'athlete's total EE from the activity in terms of METs throughout a 24-hour day is 41.25. The final step is to divide this value by the total time (hours) in which it has been estimated, to produce an hourly average MET value. Therefore, the daily EE from activity would be 41.25/24 = 1.72 METs. Remembering that 1 MET equates to the individuals BMR, we would then multiply our athlete's BMR of 1,410 kcal by the average daily METs of 1.72, for a total daily EE of 2,425 kcal. Now that we have a calculated daily EE for our e'athlete, we have gained an understanding of nutritional needs, and some knowledge of optimal nutrition timing, we can formulate a nutrition plan. Table 5.4 outlines a

Table 5.4 Example 24-hour Activity and Meal Plan for an E'athlete

Time (24 hr)	Activity	EE (METs)	Kcal equ.	Food Intake	Food Kcal
0	Readying to sleep	1.0	58.75		
1					
2					
3					
4	Sleeping	1.0 × 8 = 8	470		
5					
6					
7					
8					
9	Wake, ready, and breakfast	1.5	88.125	Meal 1	414
10	Travel to university (bus)	1.5	88.125		
11	Class	1.5 × 2 = 3	176.25	Snack 1	89
12					
13	Lunch	1.5	88.125	Meal 2	533
14	Class	1.5 × 2 = 3	176.25	Snack 2	249
15					
16	Exercise (run 45 mins @ 11 km/hr)	11.0	646.25		
17	Study at desk	1.5	88.125		
18	Cook and eat dinner	2.0	117.5	Meal 3	560
19					
20	Esports practice	2.5 × 4 = 10	587.5	Snack 3	258
21					
22					
23	Watch television	1.5	88.125	Snack 4	580
	Total	**45.5**	**2673.125**		**2,683**

	Food	Total Kcal	CHO	FAT	PRO
Meal 1	2 × scrambled eggs, 0.5 × avocado, 2 × toasted wholemeal bread w/butter + medium latte	414	44	31	21
Meal 2	Chicken Caesar Wrap (Starbucks) + medium latte	533	44	31	20
Meal 3	2 × beef sausages, 1 cup potato mash, 1 cup steamed brocoli	560	20	36	21
Snack 1	1 × medium banana	89	23	0	1
Snack 2	1 × medium appe + 1 × tub Chobani natural Greek yoghurt	249	43	3	13
Snack 3	600 mL Coke	258	64	0	0
Snack 4	2 × toasted wholemeal bread with 3 tbsp peanut butter	580	37	35	25
		2683	275	136	101

planned day for our e'athlete, including approximate waking time, planned physical activity and exercise, and an esports practice session. Outlined in the table is also the approximate EE for the planned activities, and food and meal suggestions to meet kcal deficit of daily activities, with consideration for nutrient timing around esports practice.

Depending on the professional level of the esports team/athlete, and the resources available, a team may opt for a dedicated nutrition practitioner. Of course, if this is not feasible, then the e'athlete and coaching staff can use the given information and example to guide their own nutrition planning. It is important that this planning be undertaken in consultation with the e'athlete, with considerations of readiness for behaviour change. The e'athlete education, and awareness of nutrition intake, will be of paramount benefit in building and maintaining ongoing changes to support health and performance.

5.5 Ergogenic aids and banned substances

When we think of ergogenic aids used within sport, we likely think of supplements such as raw protein, creatine, and beta-alanine. As esports performance is heavily influenced by cognition, rather than physicality, the primary supplement in use at all levels of competition is caffeine. In fact, many esports competitions and teams are sponsored by caffeinated beverage (i.e. energy drinks) companies. Caffeine is a drug which stimulates the central nervous system, which is responsible for sending and receiving chemical messages to the body. Caffeine blocks the binding of adenosine within the brain, which enhances acetylcholine release. Acetylcholine is a neurotransmitter linked to activity at the neuromuscular junction (where nerves meet muscle tissue), within the autonomic nervous system, central nervous system, and other cellular effects within the body. There is a strong base of evidence to support the positive performance impacts of caffeine within sport. Typical doses within sport range from ~2 to 4 mg.kg.bw. For a 70 kg athlete that would equate to 140–280 mg. For reference, a standard espresso coffee contains ~100 mg of caffeine, while a 473 mL can of G Fuel™ (a major sponsor of esports and video game streamers) contains 300 mg of caffeine. Evidence to support caffeine supplementation for esports performance is limited and mostly inconclusive.

While caffeine has been shown to improve cognitive elements such as reaction time, alertness, and attention (McLellan et al., 2016), as well as self-reported feelings of alertness, energy, and mood (Calvo et al., 2021), two studies looking at caffeine ingestion (2.5 mg.kg.bw) and esports performance showed no significant improvements (Thomas et al., 2019; Turner, 2023). However, Sainz and colleagues (2020) indicated that caffeine (3 mg.kg.bw) reduced reaction time for FPS e'athletes in a randomised experimental study. In a PhD thesis, Turner (2023) found that 47% of e'athletes used supplements to enhance performance in esports. Of those supplements, 85% contained caffeine, with the average pre-game dosage for elite e'athletes being 162 ± 85 mg. The most common reasons reported for caffeine supplementation were to prevent fatigue (particularly for back-to-back, or late-night games), improve energy or arousal, taste, and concentration.

Despite early findings that caffeine may not directly impact esports performance, there should be considerations for its use for fatigue prevention, mood, and alertness. As some individuals may report a negative effect from caffeine (such as anxiety or gastric stress), the use of caffeine supplementation should be a discussion had with the e'athlete alongside the health and performance coaching team. Alongside caffeine, there are other medications and drugs which are known to elicit a stimulating effect on the central nervous system. Sometimes the use of these drugs are necessary for medically-relevant reasons, while occasionally they may be illegally acquired and used for performance enhancement.

The Esports Integrity Commission (ESIC) (Esports Integrity Commission, n.d.), founded in 2016, is responsible for disruption and prevention investigating and prosecution of all forms of cheating in esports. Some of these responsibilities include investigation of potential match-fixing and cheating by e'athletes' use of banned substances (doping). Currently, there are several medications and substances identified by ESIC as potential 'performance enhancers' – that is, substances taken by e'athletes to achieve an unfair advantage over their competitors. The following substances, listed by their generic medical names, are currently prohibited in use by e'athletes when competing in a tournament governed by ESIC (for example, Dreamhack, ESL, and Allied Esports):

- Amphetamine sulfate
- Dextroamphetamine
- Dexedrine
- Dexmethylphenidate
- Lisdexamfetamine
- Methylphenidate
- Modafinil and armodafinil

As expected, the banned substance list primarily consists of stimulant class drugs. These substances have strong potential to improve cognitive function in terms of attention, information retention, and fatigue resistance (Avois et al., 2006). There is of course some cloudiness in terms of regulation of substance use and mis-use in esports. Unlike many other sports, where advantage may be unfairly gained from use of substances that enhance muscular strength, power, or fatigue resistance (such as anabolic steroids and erythropoietin) where medical therapeutic use would be considered unusual for an adult athlete, many of the substances on the ESIC banned list are commonly used in adolescents and adults for a variety of cognitive and learning therapies (such as attention deficit hyperactive disorder, narcolepsy, autism, and obsessive-compulsive disorders). Therefore, ESIC is guided by 'therapeutic use exemptions' in determining if the e'athlete has a medical necessity for the use of a stimulant (Esports Integrity Commission, n.d.), such as being prescribed by a medical professional following a formal diagnosis.

5.6 Summary

Human biochemistry and metabolism are complex processes influenced by several factors such as diet, exercise, medications, disease, injury, emotional and physical stress, and external factors like climate and altitude. Biochemistry is a fundamental topic across medical and health science degrees as it forms the basis of all biological processes within the human body. Following ingestion, macronutrients are digested into their base constituents and can follow specific metabolic pathways to assist in replenishing ATP. There are three interrelated biochemical pathways involved in ATP resynthesis, including the phosphagen system, glycolysis, and oxidative metabolism. ATP resynthesis must keep up with ATP demand to maintain homeostasis, and when ATP resynthesis can no longer match ATP demand, fatigue occurs. Efficiency of ATP resynthesis can be improved through exercise and optimal diet.

The WHO and the ACSM have recommended daily intake of fruits, vegetables, proteins, and water, and advised to limit free sugars and total energy intake from fats. Poor diet may have negative effects on cognition and memory during brain development, and athletes' receptiveness to dietary change, nutrition education, and the timeframe for nutritional programming should be considered while designing nutrition plans. Nutrient timing is also an important factor in nutrition programming, and preliminary studies suggest that meal composition and timing affect esports performance. Habits such as increasing intake of fruits and vegetables, high-quality carbs, reducing portion sizes, and regular meal patterns improve performance, while meal skipping and chronic dehydration have negative impacts.

An individual nutrition prescription for e'athletes is best achieved through understanding their needs and energy expenditure. Assessing the body composition is an important consideration in dietary programming, and physical activity is a significant contributor to daily energy expenditure. Caffeine is the primary supplement used in esports due to its positive effects on cognition, and while evidence to support caffeine supplementation for esports performance is limited, it can improve cognitive elements such as reaction time, alertness, and attention. The ESIC is responsible for investigating and prosecuting all forms of cheating in esports, including the use of banned substances such as amphetamine sulfate, dextroamphetamine, and modafinil. The ESIC considers therapeutic use exemptions when determining if a player has a medically necessary use of a stimulant.

References

Ackuaku-Dogbe, E. M., and Abaidoo, B. (2014). Breakfast eating habits among medical students. *Ghana Medical Journal*, 48(2), 66–70. https://doi.org/10.4314/gmj.v48i2.2

Adolphus, K., Lawton, C. L., Champ, C. L., and Dye, L. (2016). The effects of breakfast and breakfast composition on cognition in children and adolescents: a systematic review. *Advances in Nutrition*, 7(3), 590S–612S. https://doi.org/10.3945/an.115.010256

Ainsworth, B. E., Haskell, W. L., Whitt, M. C., Swartz, A. M., Strath, S. J., Bassett Jr, D. R., Schmitz, K. H., Emplaincourt, P. O., Jacobs Jr, D. R., and Leon, A. S. (2000). Compendium of physical activities: an update of activity codes and MET intensities. *Medicine and Science in Sports and Exercise, 32*(9), 498–504.

American College of Sports Medicine. (2011). *Protein intake for optimal muscle maintenance* [Brochure].

Arain, M., Haque, M., Johal, L., Mathur, P., Nel, W., Rais, A., Sandhu, R., and Sharma, S. (2013). Maturation of the adolescent brain. *Neuropsychiatric Disease and Treatment, 9*, 449–461.

Atherton, P. J., and Smith, K. (2012). Muscle protein synthesis in response to nutrition and exercise. *The Journal of Physiology, 590*(5), 1049–1057.

Avois, L., Robinson, N., Saudan, C., Baume, N., Mangin, P., and Saugy, M. (2006). Central nervous system stimulants and sport practice. *British Journal of Sports Medicine, 40*(Suppl 1), i16–i20. https://doi.org/10.1136/bjsm.2006.027557

Bahr, R., Ingnes, I., Vaage, O., Sejersted, O. M., and Newsholme, E. A. (1987). Effect of duration of exercise on excess post-exercise O_2 consumption. *Journal of Applied Physiology, 62*, 485–490.

Baker, J. S., McCormick, M. C., and Robergs, R. A. (2010). Interaction among skeletal muscle metabolic energy systems during intense exercise. *Journal of Nutrition and Metabolism, 2010*, 1–13. https://doi.org/10.1155/2010/905612

Bendavid, I., Lobo, D. N., Barazzoni, R., Cederholm, T., Coëffier, M., van der Schueren, M., Fontaine, E., Hiesmayr, M., Laviano, A., Pichard, C., and Singer, P. (2021). The centenary of the Harris-Benedict equations: how to assess energy requirements best? Recommendations from the ESPEN expert group. *Clinical Nutrition, 40*(3), 690–701.

Bernstein, M. S., Morabia, A., and Sloutskis, D. (1999). Definition and prevalence of sedentarism in an urban population. *American Journal of Public Health, 89*(6), 862–867.

Børsheim, E., and Bahr, R. (2003). Effect of exercise intensity, duration and mode on post-exercise oxygen consumption. *Sports Medicine, 33*, 1037–1060.

Børsheim, E., Bahr, R., Hansson, P., Gullestad, L., Hallén, J., and Sejersted, O. M. (1994). Effect of β-adrenoceptor blockade on post-exercise oxygen consumption. *Metabolism, 43*(5), 565–571.

Calvo, J. L., Fei, X., Domínguez, R., and Pareja-Galeano, H. (2021). Caffein and cognitive functions in sports: a systematic review and meta-analysis. *Nutrients, 13*(3), 868.

Champe, P. C., Harvey, R. A., and Ferrier, D. R. (2005). *Biochemistry* (3rd ed.). Lippincott Williams & Wilkins.

Douglas, C. C., Lawrence, J. C., Bush, N. C., Oster, R. A., Gower, B. A., and Darnell, B. E. (2007). Ability of the Harris Benedict formula to predict energy requirements differs with weight history and ethnicity. *Nutritional Research, 27*(4), 194–199.

Dragoo, J. L., Shapiro, S. A., Bradsell, H., and Frank, R. M. (2021). The essential roles of human adipose tissue: metabolic, thermoregulatory, cellular, and paracrine effects. *Journal of Cartilage & Joint Preservation, 1*(3), 1–9.

ESPN Stats & Info. (September, 2017). *Average age in esports vs. major sports*. ESPN. https://www.espn.com.au/esports/story/_/id/20733853/the-average-age-esports-versus-nfl-nba-mlb-nhl

Esports Integrity Commission. (n.d.). *Anti-doping code*. https://esic.gg/codes/anti-doping-code/

Gaesser, G. A., and Brooks, G. A. (1984). Metabolic bases of excess post-exercise oxygen consumption: a review. *Medicine and Science in Sports and Exercise, 16*(1), 29–43.

Gropper, S. S., and Smith, J. L. (2013). *Advanced nutrition and human metabolism* (6th ed.). Cengage Learning.

Harris, J. A., and Benedict, F. G. (1919). *A biometric study of basal metabolism in man*. Carnegie Institution of Washington.

Haskell, W. L., Lee, I., Pate, R. R., Powell, K. E., Blair, S. N., Franklin, B. A., Macera, C. A., Heath, G. W., Thompson, P. D., and Bauman, A. (2007). Physical activity and public health. *Medicine and Science in Sports and Exercise, 39*(8), 1423–1434.

Hermansen, L., Grandmontagne, M., Mæhlum, S., and Ignes, I. (1984). Postexercise elevation of resting oxygen uptake: possible mechanisms and physiological significance. In: Marconnet, P., Poortmans, J., Hermansen, L., editors. *Medicine and sport science*. Vol. 17. Karger, 119–129.

Howard, G., and Bartram, J. (2003). *Domestic water quantity, service, level and health*. World Health Organization.

Hulbert, A. J., and Else, P. L. (2004). Basal metabolic rate: history, composition, regulation, and usefulness. *Physiological and Biochemical Zoology, 77*(6), 869–876.

Jéquier, E., and Constant, F. (2010). Water as an essential nutrient: the physiological basis of hydration. *European Journal of Clinical Nutrition, 64*(2), 115–123.

Jovanovic, B. (August, 2022). *Gamer demographics: facts and stats about the most popular hobby in the world*. Dataprot. https://dataprot.net/statistics/gamer-demographics/

Kerksick, C. M., Arent, S., Schoenfeld, B. J., Stout, J. R., Campbell, B., Wilborn, C. D., Taylor, L., Kalman, D., Smith-Ryan, A. E., Kreider, R. B., Willoughby, D., Arciero, P. J., VanDusseldorp, T. A., Ormsbee, M. J., Wildman, R., Greenwood, M., Ziegenfuss, T. N., Aragon, A. A., and Antonio, J. (2017). International society of sports nutrition position stand: nutrient timing. *Journal of the International Society of Sports Nutrition, 14*, 33. https://doi.org/10.1186/s12970-017-0189-4

LaForgia, J., Withers, R. T., and Gore, C. J. (2006). Effects of exercise intensity and duration on the excess post-exercise oxygen consumption. *Journal of Sports Science, 24*(12), 1247–1264.

LaForgia, J., Withers, R. T., Shipp, N. J., and Gore, C. J. (1997). Comparison of energy expenditure elevations after submaximal and supramaximal running. *Journal of Applied Physiology, 82*, 661–666.

Mamerow, M. (2022). *Age of pro gamers – oldest – average – youngest (2022)*. Raise Your Skillz. https://raiseyourskillz.com/how-old-are-pro-gamers/

Mann, J., and Truswell, A. S. (2012). *Essentials of human nutrition* (4th ed.). Oxford University Press.

McLellan, T. M., Caldwell, J. A., and Lieberman, H. R. (2016). A review of caffeine's effects on cognitive, physical and occupational performance. *Neuroscience and Biobehavioral Reviews, 71*, 294–312.

Naveed, S., Lakka, T., and Haapala, E. A. (2020). An overview on the associations between health behaviors and brain health in children and adolescents with special reference to diet quality. *International Journal of Environmental Research and Public Health, 17*(3), 953.

Ndahimana, D., and Kim, E. (2017). Measurement methods for physical activity and energy expenditure: a review. *Clinical Nutrition Research, 6*(2), 68–80.

Nyaradi, A., Foster, J. K., Hickling, S., Li, J., Ambrosini, G. L., Jacques, A., and Oddy, W. H. (2014). Prospective associations between dietary patterns and cognitive performance during adolescence. *The Journal of Child Psychology and Psychiatry, 55*(9), 1017–1024.

Ørtenblad, N., Westerbald, H., and Nielsen, J. (2013). Muscle glycogen stores and fatigue. *The Journal of Physiology, 591*(18), 4405–4413.

Phelain, J. F., Reinke, E., Harris, M. A., and Melby, C. L. (1997). Postexercise energy expenditure and substrate oxidation in young women resulting from exercise bouts of different intensity. *Journal of the American College of Nutrition, 16*, 140–146.

Pontzer, H., Yamada, Y., Sagayama, H., Ainslie, P. N., Andersen, L. F., Anderson, L. J., Arab, L., Baddou, I., Bedu-Addo, K., Blaak, E. E., Blanc, S., Bonomi, A. G., Bouten, C. V. C., Bovet, P., Buchowski, M. S., Butte, N. F., Camps, S. G., Close, G. L., Cooper, J. A., … Speakman, J. R. (2021). Daily energy expenditure through the human life course. *Science, 373*(6556), 808–812.

Prochaska, J. O., and Velicer, W. F. (1997). The transtheoretical model of health behavior change. American Journal of Health Promotion, 12(1), 38–48. https://doi.org/10.4278/0890-1171-12.1.38

Quinn, T. J., Vroman, N. B., and Kertzer, R. (1994). Postexercise oxygen consumption in trained females: effect of exercise duration. *Medicine and Science in Sports and Exercise, 26*, 908–913.

Ravussin, E., and Bogardus, C. (1992). A brief overview of human energy metabolism and its relationship to essential obesity. *The American Journal of Clinical Nutrition, 55*(1), 242–245.

Ribeiro, F. J., Viana, V., Borges, N., and Teixeira, V. T. (2021). The emergence of esports nutrition - a review. *Central European Journal of Sport Sciences and Medicine, 33*(1), 81–95.

Sainz, I., Collado-Mateo, D., and Del Coso, J. (2020). Effect of acute caffeine intake on hit accuracy and reaction time in professional e-sports players. *Physiology & Behavior, 224*, 1–6.

Sedlock, D. A. (1991). Postexercise energy expenditure following upper body exercise. *Research Quarterly for Exercise and Sport, 62*, 213–216.

Silverman, J., Kurtz, S., and Draper, J. (2013). *Skills for Communicating with Patients* (3rd ed.). CRC Press. https://doi.org/10.1201/9781910227268

Smith, J., and McNaughton, L. (1993). The effects of intensity of exercise on excess postexercise oxygen consumption and energy expenditure in moderately trained men and women. *European Journal of Applied Physiology, 67*, 420–425.

Thomas, C. J., Rothschild, J., Earnest, C. P., and Blaisdell, A. (2019). The effects of energy drink consumption on cognitive and physical performance in elite Leage of Legneds players. *Sports (Basel), 7*(9), 196.

Thompson, D., Karpe, F., Lafontan, M., and Frayn, K. (2012). Physical activity and exercise in the regulation of human tissue physiology. *Physiological Reviews, 92*(1), 157–191.

Turner, J. (2023). *Exploring the role of dietary intake and supplementation on performance in video gaming and esports* [Unpublished doctoral dissertation]. Queensland University of Technology.

World Health Organization. (April, 2020). *Healthy diet* [Fact sheet]. World Health Organization. https://www.who.int/news-room/fact-sheets/detail/healthy-diet

World Health Organization. (2005). *Nutrients in drinking water.* Sustainable Development and Healthy Environments Cluster.

6 Social aspects of e'athletes performance

Remco Polman and Kabir Bubna

6.1 Social factors influencing health, well-being, and performance in e'athletes

Whereas sport psychology mainly deals with individual characteristics and determinants of health, psychological well-being, and performance, social psychology deals with group processes like working in a team, communication, and the coach–e'athlete relationship. Like traditional sports, even in those esports in which one competes individually often others are involved which influence well-being and success. This could be coaches, support staff (psychologists, nutritionists, or physical trainer) or significant others like parents and peers. In a recent scoping review, it was argued that the most important factors for success are teamwork and cooperation related skills and not the development of e'athletes personal attributes and skills (Sanz-Matesanz et al., 2023). This is not surprising considering that teamwork in traditional sport has also been shown to result in higher efficiency and productivity (Carron et al., 2005). As such, it is imperative that to achieve e'athletes' true potential, it is important to develop teamworking skills. This is also reflected in many slogans used in traditional sports which are often displayed in dressing rooms like 'we won as a team', 'there is no I in team', and 'TEAM: Together Everyone Achieves More' (Polman et al., 2018).

6.2 Team cohesion

Many coaches spent much time in identifying and developing talented e'athletes. In addition, much of the training and coaching is geared towards the development of individual skills and abilities. However, the best individual e'athletes are not necessarily making the best team. Numerous examples from traditional sport demonstrate that the team with the most talented players do not automatically become the champions. This phenomenon is called the Ringelmann effect and has been attributed to complications in co-ordination and motivational processes. In addition, currently e-sports teams seem to be in regular flux by changing teammates on a regular basis. However, to be successful and to achieve the potential of (talented) e'athletes, it is important to develop efficient and harmonious groups and team-work strategies. This will reduce internal challenges and disruption which

DOI: 10.4324/9781003322382-6

can annihilate teams and improve unity and the likelihood of success as well as satisfaction of the e'athletes (Janssen, 1999).

A factor identified to enhance teamwork is team cohesion. Cohesion or 'cohesiveness' is defined as "how members all work together for a common goal, or where everyone is ready to take responsibility for group chores (Cartwright, 1968, p. 70). According to Carron (1982), team cohesion consists of two factors: (1) Individual attraction to the group and (2) group integration (bonding within a group). Importantly, both group attraction and integration have a social and task component. Task cohesion focusses on how members of the team can work together and maintain unity while achieving group objectives, whereas social cohesion refers to the willingness of members within a group to create interpersonal relationships, and if they enjoy the company of their teammates (Al-Yaaribi & Kavussanu, 2017; Beal et al., 2003). The theory suggests that e'athletes stay in a team either for social aspects (friendship) or team goals (winning a particular championship) or both.

Of course, it is important to understand what factors drives team cohesion. Unfortunately, there is no esports-specific research on this issue to date, however, work conducted in sport teams suggests that team stability is related to cohesion. Teams with regular turnover or absence (e.g., because of injury of illness) are less likely to develop cooperation and don't stick together. Trust and support have also been found to improve cohesion (De Jong et al., 2016; Swettenham & Whitehead, 2022). In addition, Wann (1997) identified that team cohesion was influenced by the development of team identity through rules and behaviours (e.g., dress code, time keeping) and communication patterns. Of course, it is more difficult to establish team cohesion in larger groups because of increased difficulties to coordinate activities and communicate effectively (Widmeyer et al., 1990). Access to facilities and resources and individual contracts (and the discrepancies between e'athletes) are also likely to influence team cohesion (Carron & Hausenblas, 1998). Not surprisingly, personal factors and coaching behaviours can also influence team cohesion. Increased levels of sacrifice behaviour, social-loafing, and self-handicapping have been found to influence team cohesion negatively. Whereas coaches who involve athletes in decision-making processes and are perceived as committed and complementary contribute to enhancing team cohesion (Jowett & Chaundy, 2004).

Ultimately, team cohesion is a vital component for development and performance and well-being in both team and individual esports. However, it is important to remember, although synergies and cohesion can emerge spontaneously, it is more likely to be developed and shaped over time as members of the team continue to interact with each other (Kozlowski & Chao, 2012; Mathieu et al., 2015).

Meta-analysis has shown that here is strong evidence that increased levels of team cohesion (social and task) is associated with higher performance in both sport (Carron et al., 2002) and other domains (Mullen & Copper, 1994). Interestingly, women's teams show a stronger association than men's teams. In addition, the effect for professional teams has been lower in comparison to high school and intercollegiate teams. However, this is mainly due to few studies being conducted in professional teams. Cross-lagged panel studies have also tried to establish whether success leads to increased cohesion or vice versa. By assessing team cohesion and performance at multiple times during the season, it has been shown that the association between early success and later team cohesion is stronger compared to team cohesion early in the season and later success. This would indicate that both are important (Boone et al., 1997).

So, what strategies could esports teams implement to become more successful but also enhance the e'athletes' physical and psychosocial wellbeing? Team-building activities have been developed and used in many settings with the aim of developing individual responsibility to achieve team goals. In line with the theory of team cohesion presented earlier, such team building exercises can influence task and social aspects (Carron et al., 2005). Polman et al. (2018) have previously presented a list of strategies which have been adapted for esports:

1 *Foster feelings of ownership:* By involving the e'athletes in day-to-day activities and decision making they are more likely feel part of the team.
2 *Enhance team self-efficacy*: Based on Bandura's (1986) social cognitive theory higher levels of team efficacy will lead to increased performance. This could be achieved through being successful (success leads to increased levels of self-efficacy), communication by the coach about the abilities of the team and observing why other teams are successful.
3 *Role acceptance*: E'athletes should all feel that they have a unique and important contribution to make to the success of the team.
4 *Practice exercises to promote cooperation*: Make the e'athletes aware of the significance of depending on their teammates for success. For example, the e'athletes could exercise or prepare meals together.
5 *There will be conflict*: Even in successful teams there will be conflict; it is just important to manage this in a positive way. The absence of conflict might indicate lack of commitment and result in poor performance.
6 *Cliques*: E'athletes and coach can develop cliques within a team. For example, coaches might use scapegoats or favourites whereas the e'athletes might develop sub-groups. Overall, cliques in teams undermine group cohesion and psychological well-being and performance.
7 *Personal information*: Group cohesion is enhanced if coaches and teammates know and are aware of personal aspects of e'athletes. This could include simple things like remembering a birthday or the name of their partner and children.

Another way to enhance team cohesion is to foster social support. Because social support has many dimensions this will be discussed in the next section.

6.3 Social support

Social support is the material or emotional support an e'athlete receives from others (e.g., family, friends, teammates, or coach) and has been found an important predictor of physical health, psychological well-being, and performance in sport (Freeman & Rees, 2008). Social support is multidimensional in nature, and it is thought that the quality of the support provided is more important than the quantity.

There are several models of social support. One such model suggests that social support can be categorised as either structural (i.e., social networks and its interactions) or functional support (i.e., emotional, esteem, informational, tangible) (Freeman, 2020). Functional support can be the actual received support from others or perceived support (access to social support when required).

An important function of social support is that it can protect e'athletes from the negative consequences of stress. Cohen and Wills (1985) have suggested that social support can have a direct effect on performance as well as an indirect effect through stress buffering. Unfortunately, there is currently little empirical evidence in esports on the potential direct and indirect effects of social support on performance. However, there is some evidence from traditional sports that social support can have negative consequences. This has been shown with overburdening parents causing athletes to drop-out. In addition, the absence of social support can also have negative consequences. The role of the family in the provision of social support might be an interesting topic for future esports research in terms of too much or too little.

Madden and Harteveld (2021) recently suggested that communities can help in improving the psychological well-being of e'athletes by providing social support in dealing with stress and pressure. Although the authors acknowledge that the current structure and organisation of esports make it difficult to have access to formal support networks. Hence, in contrast to the organisation of sport in clubs in many countries, esports are often played online with relatively little human interactions. Some research has suggested that this organisational structure and lack of human interaction lead to feelings of isolation and toxic online behaviours (more about this is discussed later in this chapter). In one of the quantitative studies on social support in esports Trotter et al. (2021), using the Athletes Received Support Questionnaire (ARSQ; Freeman et al., 2014), compared e'athletes with sport athletes. They found that the e'athletes received significantly less esteem, emotional, and tangible support but similar informational support in comparison to sport athletes. These findings are to some extent in line with those of Freeman and Wohn (2019). They suggest that informational and tangible support are the foundations for esteem and emotional support in esports. In many esports, in-built match-making systems allocate teammates. When competing with complete strangers, it is not surprising that the provision of information is an important form of social support. Trotter et al. (2021) suggest that in-game pings are a good way to provide informational support thereby enhancing e'athletes' situational awareness. It is only when e'athletes continue to play together that emotional and esteem support can be provided. Considering the importance of social support to well-being (e.g., stress-buffering) and performance, it will be important for e'athletes to have access to or receive support when required either online or face to face. This might require changes in the organisational structure of esports and the development of more developmental or grassroots esports programs.

6.4 Communication in esports

In Chapter 4 we deliberately created a high discrepancy score for communication in the performance profiling section. In most esports, the only way to communicate is through verbal language. This is because you often can't see your teammates (or opponent) making it impossible to use non-verbal communication. With teamwork and cooperation-related skills identified as the most important elements to enhance performance (Sanz-Matesanz et al., 2023), it is apparent that clear and effective communication is required to improve team dynamics and group cohesion (Tan et al., 2022). Communication can have different forms and can be between the coach and e'athletes or among e'athletes themselves. It can be discussions about performance (during training and competition) or about personal issues. To enhance communication, it is important to improve the effectiveness of messages and decrease miscommunication.

In game communication allows information to be exchanged between teammates through implicit (non-verbal) and explicit (verbal) means (Lausic, 2009; Marlow et al., 2018). Verbal communication is conducted through various available software (i.e., Discord, Skype, Teamspeak). Within verbal communication channels, teams not only focus on task-related elements like planning, preparation, and coordination but also facilitate social cohesion by expressing frustration or providing praise and feedback. Verbal channels allow information related to performance to be efficiently transferred and also establish interpersonal/team relationships, allowing attention to be maintained to enhance situational awareness. Non-verbal channels are also frequently used within each respective esports. These are more commonly referred to as 'pings' (i.e., temporary, visual, and audio cues) which primarily serve the function of directing attention to specific areas of the game, allowing for reinforcement of verbal communication channels.

Strategies to improve in-game communication might be to shorten communication (focus on one thing at a time) and use codes to disguise messages. Using the name of the individual you want to communicate with is more likely to grab their attention in addition be consistent (what you want now is the same as what you wanted yesterday) and frame your message in a positive way (Janssen, 1999). For example, telling somebody not to do something might have the opposite effect. This is called ironic processing. Finally, sometimes it is important to establish whether your teammates have understood your messages. Other strategies involve listening, trying to understand your teammates' perspective (being empathetic), learn how to provide and receive feedback in a constructive way, and accepting team members for who they are (e.g., Eccles & Tran, 2012; Yukelson, 2008).

6.5 Coach-athlete relationship

The presence of coaches and now the act of coaching is becoming a more regular feature across the esports industry and are present at every level of participation from grassroots to professional (Hedlund et al., 2020; Himmelstein et al., 2017). Coaches play a key role in providing support that scaffolds the development and well-being of athletes in any context, therefore, it is equally important to consider the coach–athlete relationship as a crucial factor to success. This dyadic relationship formed between the coach and athlete is always unique, and it is said that both need to support each other for success in performance contexts (Jowett & Shanmugam, 2016).

Jowett (2009) developed a model that measured the quality of core dimensions shared between a coach and athlete. The 3+1Cs model views the coach–athlete relationship as a social situation, where their affective states (i.e., feelings and emotions), will influence their cognition (i.e., thoughts) and subsequently their behavioural interactions with one another. The original '3Cs' of the model include constructs of Closeness, Commitment, and Complementarity. Closeness refers to the affective connection developed by people in any relationship. Development of trust, respect, and appreciation of each other is key to achieving closeness. Commitment describes the intention for individuals to want to maintain the bond and continue to work effectively with their peers. Lastly, complementarity aligns itself with effective and cooperative interactions between the coach and athlete. It reflects the affiliated motivation of interpersonal behaviours and encompasses acts such as being responsive, friendly, at ease, open to feedback, and willing. The '+1Cs' refers to co-orientation. This describes the similarities and degree of alignment that may exist between a coach and athlete. It also includes the coaches' perceptions on the quality of their working relationship.

Coaches who work on the original 3Cs open the door to developing genuine relationships with their athletes, which can build an environment where honesty, trust, and effective communication is valued. Developing a positive coach–athlete relationship also allows athletes to face personal growth, which can positively impact them as they transition out of competitive participation into their future endeavours. Lastly, by modelling positive relationships to players, it can help them take on mentoring roles to younger/newer players with the team or provide a foundation for players if they decide themselves to transition into a coaching/management role.

6.6 Choking under pressure

There are numerous examples of e'athletes or teams who, despite being motivated and expecting to win, fail miserably and perform way below their capabilities. This is referred to as choking and is most likely to happen when there is substantial pressure to win. There have been several theories on why performers might choke under pressure. One such theory was proposed by Masters, Polman, and Hammond (1993; see also Masters & Maxwell, 2008). They suggested that choking is associated with self-focussed behaviour (Mor & Winquist, 2002). Masters et al. (1993) reinvestment theory states that performers under situations of high stress will start to pay conscious attention to how to execute the motor skill at hand. Conscious motor skill execution is associated with the early stages of the learning process (called the cognitive stage) and is generally slow, erratic, explicit, and full of errors. This works in contrast when a motor skill is mastered (autonomous phase). At this stage of the learning process, motor skill execution is fast, fluent, implicit, and errorless. Conscious attention to the execution of motor skills interferes with normal automatic control of performance and can have disastrous consequences. For example, the act of walking down the stairs is an easy task for most and can be completed without any thoughts. However, if you try to walk down the stairs and start to think about how your legs are moving, it suddenly becomes very difficult and you must be careful not to fall down the stairs. Introspection of the motor task at hand is much more likely to result in failure. The tendency to reinvest (an inward focus of attention in which an attempt is made to perform the skill online via working memory) is seen as a personality trait with those high in this trait more likely to choke in situations of high stress.

Baumeister (1984), on the other hand, proposed an opposing theory. His acclimatisation hypothesis suggests that those high in the personality trait self-consciousness are least likely to be affected by high-stress situations. In this view those performers who are not used to experiencing self-consciousness are likely to choke under pressure whereas those high in self-consciousness on a regular basis don't experience this as interfering.

The tendency to overthink technique or focus on aspects of performance which might help to improve performance has the paradoxical effect of reducing performance (Masters & Maxwell, 2008). When the e'athlete experiences high levels of stress or is being evaluated by others (e.g., audience), this can cause reinvestment. An interesting strategy which has the potential to increase self-consciousness and reinvestment is to praise your opponent (Potter, 1947 cited in Masters & Maxwell, 2008).

6.7 Toxicity in esports

Although esports provides a platform for a range of positive development for individuals, behind the anonymity of the internet, toxic social interaction is something everyone will witness (Wu et al., 2021). Toxicity is when a communication channel (in-game chat feature, voice channels) is abused for the sole purpose of harassment of other players, which goes against the inclusive code of esports.

6.7.1 Solo queue

Solo queue is a prominent feature in every competitive esports title. It provides a platform for players to compete, hone their skills, and climb the ladder with ambitions to reach desired ranks that hold social capital. However, within solo queue, players are matched randomly with other players with a similar match-making rating (MMR). These teams are ad-hoc, and therefore, the interaction between players is usually very short, with many never playing alongside or against each other again. This can encourage toxic behaviour as players might demand the best from their teammates in every game, as winning or losing can be beneficial or hinder rank progression (Wagner, 2006; Witowski, 2012).

For players who struggle or fail to regulate their emotions, they are susceptible to abusing communications channels and engaging in toxic behaviour (e.g., pointing out teammates' mistakes, excessive typing, and verbal abuse) which are all signs that an individual might be experiencing 'tilt' (overwhelming negative emotions or frustration; Wu et al., 2021). Tilt can also induce other 'anti-social' behaviour, where players will purposefully play worse either by giving kills for free to the opponents, (intentionally feeding, also known as 'inting') or not playing with the team, which consequently deters the teams' ability to effectively compete (grieving). Lastly, players can also go away from the keyboard (AFK), which means they either sit idle in the game not contributing or completely disconnect from the game, which greatly hinders the chances for a team to win due to the numerical disadvantage.

6.7.2 Team conflict

Team conflict is an inevitable part of every competitive team's history. How teams navigate it becomes the true challenge and ultimately shapes the team for success or failure. Team conflict can arise for a plethora of reasons (e.g., frustrations about individual/team performance, not achieving expectations of the team, and not complying with the teams' standards/values). Conflicts usually happen because players will have their own beliefs on what the best course of action is, and because players refine their skills within a solo queue environment, they lack the effective communication skills to convey their core message across, which can lead to unproductive discussions. Within esports, a large part of the coaching role is to be a mediator within these interpersonal conflicting discussions to allow players to share opinions, debate ideas, and collaboratively develop courses for action for the future of the team.

References

Al-Yaaribi, A., & Kavussanu, M. (2017). Teammate prosocial and antisocial behaviors predict task cohesion and burnout: The mediating role of affect. *Journal of Sport and Exercise Psychology, 39*(3), 199–208.

Bandura (1986). *Social foundations of thought and action: A social cognitive theory*. Englewood Cliffs, NJ: Prentice Hall.

Baumeister, R. F. (1984). Choking under pressure: Self-consciousness and paradoxical effects of incentives on skillful performance. *Journal of Personality and Social Psychology, 46*, 610–620.

Beal, D. J., Cohen, R. R., Burke, M. J., & McLendon, C. L. (2003). Cohesion and performance in groups: A meta-analytic clarification of construct relations. *Journal of Applied Psychology, 88*(6), 989.

Boone, K. S., Beiter, P., & Kuhlman, J. S. (1997). The effect of the win/loss record on cohesion. *Journal of Sport Behavior, 20*(2), 125–134.

Carron, A. V. (1982). Cohesiveness in sport groups: Interpretations and considerations. *Journal of Sport Psychology, 4*(2), 123–138.

Carron, A. V., Colman, M. M., Wheeler, J., & Stevens, D. (2002). Cohesion and performance in sport: A meta-analysis. *Journal of Sport & Exercise Psychology, 24*(2), 168–188.

Carron, A. V., & Hausenblas, H. A. (1998). *Group dynamics in sport* (2nd ed.). Morgantown, WV: Fitness Information Technology.

Carron, A. V., Hausenblas, H. A., & Eys, M. A. (2005). *Group dynamics in sport* (3rd ed.). Morgantown, WV: Fitness Information Technology.

Cartwright, D. (1968). The nature of group cohesiveness. *Group Dynamics: Research and Theory, 91*, 109.

Cohen, S., & Wills, T. A. (1985). Stress, social support, and the buffering hypothesis. *Psychological Bulletin, 98*(2), 310–357.

de Jong, B. A., Dirks, K. T., & Gillespie, N. (2016). Trust and team performance: A meta-analysis of main effects, moderators, and covariates. *Journal of Applied Psychology, 101*(8), 1134.

Eccles, D. W., & Tran, K. B. (2012). Getting them on the same page: Strategies for enhancing coordination and communication in sports teams. *Journal of Sport Psychology in Action, 3*, 30–40.

Freeman, P. (2020). Social support in sport. In G. Tenenbaum & R. C. Eklund (Eds.), *Handbook of sport psychology* (1st ed., pp. 447–463). New York: Wiley.

Freeman, P., Coffee, P., Moll, T., Rees, T., & Sammy, N. (2014). The ARSQ: The athlete's' received support questionnaire. *Journal of Sport & Exercise Psychology, 36*, 189–202.

Freeman, P., & Rees, T. (2008). The effects of perceived and received support on objective performance outcome. *European Journal of Sport Science, 8*, 359–368.

Freeman, P., & Wohn, D. Y. (2019). Understanding esports team formation and coordination. *Computer Supported Cooperated Work, 28*, 95–126.

Hedlund, D., Fried, G., & Smith, R. (Eds.). (2020). *Esports business management*. Champaign, IL: Human Kinetics Publishers.

Himmelstein, D., Liu, Y., & Shapiro, J. L. (2017). An exploration of mental skills among competitive league of legend players. *International Journal of Gaming and Computer-Mediated Simulations, 9*(2), 1–21.

Janssen, J. (1999). *Championship team building: What every coach needs to know to build a motivated, committed & Cohesive team*. Tucson, AZ: Winning the Mental Game.

Jowett, S. (2009). Validating coach-athlete relationship measures with the nomological network. *Measurement in Physical Education and Exercise Science, 13*(1), 34–51.

Jowett, S., & Chaundy, V. (2004). An investigation into the impact of coach leadership and coach-athlete relationship on group cohesion. *Group Dynamics: Theory, Research, and Practice, 8*(4), 302–311.

Jowett, S., & Shanmugam, V. (2016). Relational coaching in sport: Its psychological underpinnings and practical effectiveness. In R. J. Schinke, K. R. McGannon, & B. Smith (Eds.), *Routledge international handbook of sport psychology* (pp. 471–484). London: Routledge.

Kozlowski, S. W., & Chao, G. T. (2012). The dynamics of emergence: Cognition and cohesion in work teams. *Managerial and Decision Economics, 33*(5–6), 335–354.

Lausic, D. (2009). *Explicit and implicit types of communication: A conceptualization of intra-team communication in the sport of tennis*. Tallahassee: The Florida State University.

Madden, D., & Harteveld, C. (2021). Constant pressure of having to perform: Exploring player health concerns in esports. In *CHI Conference on Human Factors in Computing Systems*, May 8–13, Yokohama, Japan.

Marlow, S. L., Lacerenza, C. N., Paoletti, J., Burke, C. S., & Salas, E. (2018). Does team communication represent a one-size-fits-all approach: A meta-analysis of team communication and performance. *Organizational Behavior and Human Decision Processes, 144*, 145–170.

Masters, R., & Maxwell, J. (2008). The theory of reinvestment. *International Review of Sport and Exercise Psychology, 1*, 160–183.

Masters, R. S. W., Polman, R. C. J., & Hammond, H. V. (1993). "Reinvestment": A dimension of personality implicated in skill breakdown under pressure. *Personality and Individual Differences, 14*, 655–666.

Mathieu, J. E., Kukenberger, M. R., D'Innocenzo, L., & Reilly, G. (2015). Modelling reciprocal team cohesion–performance relationships, as impacted by shared leadership and members' competence. *Journal of Applied Psychology, 100*(3), 713.

Mor, N., & Winquist, J. (2002). Self-focused attention and negative affect: A meta-analysis. *Psychological Bulletin, 128*, 638–662.

Mullen, B., & Copper, C. (1994). The relation between group cohesiveness and performance: An integration. *Psychological Bulletin, 115*(2), 210–227.

Polman, R. C. J., Borkoles, E., & Sanchez, X. (2018). Social psychological perspective on promoting sport activities and enhancing performance in sport (Chapter 16). In L. Steg, K. E. Keizer, & A. P. Buunk (Eds.), *Applied social psychology: Understanding and managing social problems* (2nd ed., pp. 342–360). Oxford: Oxford University Press.

Sanz-Matesanz, M., Geao-Garcia, G. M., & Martinez-Aranda, L. M. (2023). Physical and psychological factors related to player's health and performance in esports: A scoping review. *Computers in Human Behavior, 143*, 107698.

Swettenham, L., & Whitehead, A. (2022). Working in esports: Developing team cohesion. *Case Studies in Sport and Exercise Psychology, 6*(1), 36–44.

Tan, E. T., Rogers, K., Nacke, L. E., Drachen, A., & Wade, A. (2022). Communication sequences indicate team cohesion: A mixed-methods study of ad hoc League of Legends teams. *Proceedings of the ACM on Human-Computer Interaction, 6*, 1–27.

Trotter, M. G., Coulter, T. J., Davis, P. A., Poulus, D. R., & Polman, R. (2021). Social support, self-regulation, and psychological skill use in e-athletes. *Frontiers in Psychology, 12*, 722030.

Wagner, M. G. (2006). On the scientific relevance of eSports. In *International Conference on Internet Computing*, June 26–29 (pp. 437–442), CSREA Press, Las Vegas.

Wann, D. L. (1997). *Sport psychology*. Upper Saddle River, NJ: Prentice Hall.

Widmeyer, W. M., Brawley, L. R., & Carron, A. V. (1990). The effects of group size in sport. *Journal of Sport and Exercise Psychology, 12*, 177–190.

Witkowski, E. (2012). On the digital playing field: How we "do sport" with networked computer games. *Games and Culture, 7*(5), 349–374.

Wu, M., Lee, J. S., & Steinkuehler, C. (2021, May). Understanding tilt in esports: A study on young league of legends players. In *Proceedings of the 2021 CHI Conference on Human Factors in Computing Systems*, May 8–13 (pp. 1–9). Yokohama, Japan.

Yukelson, D. (2008). Principles of effective team building interventions in sport: A direct service approach at Penn State University. *Journal of Applied Sport Psychology, 9*(1), 73–96.

7 Structure of esports performance environments

Matthew Watson

7.1 Introduction

We'll now turn our attention to the settings in which esports players and teams train and compete. This is an interesting area to explore given that much of the training and competition in esports takes place online, usually between opponents who are geographically separate and often involving teams whose own players are decentralised. Groups of players have been competing online, as teams or clans, in various games since the early years of esports (Wagner, 2006), and leadership in online multiplayer games has inspired research from a range of disciplines (Lisk et al., 2012). These aspects of esports are clearly distinct from traditional sport, and may have even offered useful insights for sports teams in terms of maintaining a close-knit team during the COVID-19 pandemic, during which time teams were often required to move online due to lockdown and social distancing rules (Hurley, 2021). However, within online esports environments, there are a number of challenges and contextual differences worth mentioning, and of course, there are further considerations when esports takes place "offline" at big events and finals competitions. We'll explore some of these points in the following sections.

7.2 The online esports environment

In terms of the online esports environment, the most obvious facet is the games themselves, in which players compete with and against other players and through which some communication is possible. For example, in League of Legends (LoL), e'athletes can communicate with each other through text before the game starts during the champion select phase, and in-game through similar means. For e'athletes playing in a party (i.e., two to five players), they have the option to connect to an in-built voice chat system known as League Voice. This feature is only available for those who are entering a game as a pre-set group, with no feature as of yet to invite those external to their party. However, the quality and means of communication within games themselves are limited and other tools such as Discord or Teamspeak are used to provide audio and video (i.e., face-to-face) communication channels and functions such as screen sharing. For readers unfamiliar with these platforms, it's necessary to clarify that teams will train in their own private

DOI: 10.4324/9781003322382-7

servers on these platforms, thus preventing opponents from overhearing. This is necessary as teams usually scrim (practice) against opponents they are likely to face in official competition and do not carry sufficient reserve players to train 'in house' as is commonplace in sport (Abbott et al., 2022). Interestingly, teams in different esports may have a preference for different platforms. Teamspeak, for example, may be favoured amongst Counter-Strike: Global Offensive (CS:GO) teams due to its quality, speed, and (low) system load.

7.2.1 Challenges of existing solely online

Whilst digital platforms like Discord and Teamspeak enable a higher quality of training for esports teams, teams that exist solely online are still faced with a variety of challenges. For example, though both audio and video communication are offered on these platforms, webcams are not always available (they don't tend to be standard on gaming monitors), and players are not always motivated to use them. In the absence of non-verbal body language, team communication can be somewhat impoverished, which can hinder progress in various important aspects of group dynamics (e.g., building rapport; Holt & Strean, 2001). Furthermore, teams that exist and meet solely online usually have fewer opportunities for spontaneous, unstructured interactions as a result of logging on/off at the click of a button as a training or competitive event begins/finishes. These instances or "corridor conversations" have been examined in other fields (e.g., education) and can offer individuals (e.g., players) a space to discretely discuss a personal or professional challenge, seek reassurance and learn from peers (Thomson & Trigwell, 2018). Similarly, when working remotely, esports coaches may have restricted opportunities to read and understand the political landscape within their organisation and "manage upwards" in order to secure greater support or resources for their team (Cruickshank & Collins, 2015). Other challenges to teams that operate solely online are internet connection/stability and quality, which will be discussed in Chapter 10.

7.2.2 Benefits of existing solely online

To speak briefly of the benefits, an online team of course faces a reduced financial burden as they do not need to pay for physical premises to train and accommodate players, as well as a host of associated logistic and administrative issues such as arranging visas for international players. By remaining digital and global, teams are able to take advantage of a larger talent pool (although some leagues do stipulate a domestic player minimum) and bring together players and coaches from different regions to train and compete on a regular basis. Competitions for teams like these will be hosted online through various accredited or non-accredited tournament organisers. For e'athletes, playing remotely allows them to remain in familiar surroundings, which can be an advantage when a team roster is assembled at the last minute and physically relocating – often to a new country and culture – could be a distraction or source of stress.

7.2.3 Offline and in-person

Of course, esports does not exist solely online and there are numerous high-profile annual events that take place in-person in front of both live and online audiences. As an example, 24 teams were invited to the 2022 League of Legends World Championship held in Mexico and the United States and set a record of over 5.1 million concurrent viewers (Esports Charts, 2022). Whilst these events are often the pinnacle of a player's competitive calendar and exciting for the experience alone, performing on stage can intensify performance pressure. This is not unlike professional or elite sporting competitions and leagues where athletes perform in front of thousands of spectators in arenas or stadiums, and is often televised regionally or globally. With both elite esports and sport, there is consideration of the impact of performance pressures through the application of e'athlete/athlete psychological preparation, and psychological intervention where needed during a competitive season. However, and generally speaking, some key differences exist between sport and esports in terms of mental preparedness, especially for those entering the elite/professional scene for the first time. In sport, athletes who are entering into high-level or professional competitions with large spectator numbers and live broadcasting often have prior experience with both (albeit, perhaps smaller spectator numbers and/or restricted broadcasts). Even from the very early stages of many athlete's sporting lives, they have competed in front of spectators. Perhaps these were friends and family in the early years, progressing to increasing spectator numbers as their talent and training saw them performing at increasingly competitive levels. Likely, many sports athletes have had to develop methods to cope with performance anxiety at many levels of their career, from sporting events as a child, all the way up to their professional careers. Perhaps family, friends, or coaches initially aided in mental preparation before events, or after a loss or poor performance. This may have continued across many years of development of their sporting careers, involving different approaches to mental training through exposure to different teams and coaches. With esports, many of the top-tier e'athletes of today likely began playing in solo-queues as children or teenagers, without the benefits of a consistent team or coaching staff (Abbott et al., 2022). Often, this would be the environment until the e'athlete was identified as a professional/elite prospect and recruited into a competitive team. Given the online and remote nature of esports titles played during the early stages of a promising e'athlete's life, there are years (even decades) of missed opportunity for psychological development in terms of performance pressures in esports. Without engagement with coaches or external support to develop mental preparedness through childhood and teen years, e'athletes are often faced with these pressures for the first time once they enter the early stages of their professional careers. The lack of prior experience in front of spectators, the absence of psychological training prior to the beginning of a professional career, and the relatively short period of preparation before competition begins, may all contribute to some e'athletes being less well-equipped to manage the pressures expected at highly competitive levels.

In sport, elite athletes describe how high-profile tournaments (e.g., the Olympic Games) can increase feelings of pressure and present various challenges, including distractions such as changes to the competition schedule or problems with accommodation (Arnold & Sarkar, 2015). As such, to ensure the best experience and outcome possible when competing in LAN events, e'athletes – and those working with them – are encouraged to think carefully about their preparation for the event. Drawing again from sport we know that planning is a major component of tournament preparation (Pilgrim et al., 2018), often involving goal-setting (e.g., what is the desired tournament result, optimsing psychological state) and creating a systematic plan that encompasses sport-specific strategy but also more holistic (e.g., how to minimise fatigue after long-haul travel) and practical components (e.g., familiarising oneself with the competition conditions). Much of these same ideas can be successfully applied to esports. In Box 7.1, Sport & Exercise Psychologist Callum Abbott describes some tips for ensuring that players are prepared as best as possible for a LAN tournament.

Box 7.1   Tips to ensure players feel prepared for a LAN tournament

Sport & Exercise Psychologist Callum Abbott of Team Endpoint shares some tips to ensure players feel prepared for a LAN tournament:

1 Preparation is key and should start as early as possible, especially for in-person tournaments given how different the experience is to online competition. The Sport & Exercise Psychologist and coaching staff have a key role here to ensure players are prepared. For example, the sport psychologist could work with the coach to develop pressure training scenarios to help prepare players for performing in front of a crowd, or introduce simulation training that replicates expected tournament conditions. This could involve playing crowd noise through the headsets or bringing in friends and family to watch training sessions.
2 If > Then planning: The sport psychologist can work with players and the coach to create and resolve If > Then scenarios, a psychological strategy that is useful for contingency planning. For example, if a player's keyboard and mouse setup could be lost during travel, then we will bring a spare set with us that they are familiar with to avoid them playing with unfamiliar equipment.
3 Familiarisation with the environment: If possible, take opportunities to familiarise the team with the environment (e.g., arena, studio) they will be playing in so they can prepare for things such as bright stage lights, temperature, and the general feel of the venue. If you have players that have never competed at a LAN tournament before or at that particular venue, you may also want to arrange a talk with someone who's been there before.
4 Routines and debriefs: It can be easy to be swept up in the atmosphere of a LAN environment, so encouraging a routine that involves players

checking-in with each other, the coach, and the sport psychologist can be useful to remind players of key focus points and help manage emotions. Emphasise where possible the importance of maintaining pre-performance routines and sleeping habits, as these may be impacted by travel/atmosphere/logistics at the venue.

5 On a similar note, anticipate that anything that could be different about the setups players will be using, will be different. Depending on the facilities available at the venue, players from different teams may have to take it in turns to practise on the PCs or consoles, which means settings are likely to be changed frequently. To easily avoid any stress relating to this, I recommend that before players leave their home setup they take a photo, write down every setting they use even if they don't think it's important. This includes in-game settings, monitor settings itself, and display settings on the pc (Nvidia/Amd graphics settings), etc. A quick check as part of the standard pre-performance routine can avoid surprises once the competition is underway and it's too late to make changes.

6 Finally, for the support staff, be a piece of the puzzle, not the whole puzzle. It can be easy to feel the pressure to have an answer for everything, or to overstep from a supporting role into a more active coaching role, however it is important to remember you're part of a larger puzzle of performance support for the team and whilst you are an important part of this, you cannot influence or fix everything.

7.3 In-person training environments

In certain circumstances, particularly at the highest level of competition, teams will also train together in an office setting or even live together in a gaming house (Pereira et al., 2016). For some e'athletes, moving into these situations may be a new experience on many fronts, for example, it may be their first time travelling abroad or living with peers rather than family. In recent years, the biggest organisations and brands have started investing in large training facilities that feature state-of-the-art equipment and spaces for their teams to training collaboratively within. These spaces often provide access to multidisciplinary support staff such as nutritionists or dietitians, chefs, strength and conditioning coaches, psychologists, and even physical activity areas such as a gym. When it comes to the gaming house model, there are benefits in that players get to socialise with their team mates in their free time, promoting social cohesiveness and team bonding (Pereira et al., 2016). Opportunities for both in-depth discussions and conversations among players away from the team also help to facilitate understanding, build close relationships, and develop life skills, especially when initiated by veteran players as positive examples to younger or newer players. Equally, for the coaches, sharing a physical training space with additional facilities (e.g., for eating and socialising) can offer various avenues through which to foster a positive team atmosphere

(Pedraza-Ramirez et al., 2019). However, teams should be cognisant that living in close quarter with teammates can lead to situations in which there is little work-life balance, and interpersonal conflicts are exacerbated without an opportunity to 'escape'. It may also require staff to be more aware of their professional role, identity, ethics, and safeguarding responsibilities as increased time together (especially of a social nature) may foster a sense of friendship with players (Watson et al., 2022).

7.4 The impact of the competitive structure

At higher levels of play, players are involved in competition for a significant portion of a year. This is not dissimilar to some sporting leagues which see teams, such as those in European football, competing for the majority of a calendar year. See Table 7.1 for the competitive schedules of tier-1 LoL teams if they were to play all possible games in a calendar year, which would involve competition from spring through to winter.

However, it's not just the top-tier teams that face challenges as a result of the structure of competitive leagues. Figure 7.1 displays a timeline for a single LoL split in a major European Regional League (ERL), in which some teams may have players training together in-person or choose to adopt the remote/online model. The challenge of this schedule is the pressure to 'get up and running' soon after signing a roster (indicated in the figure by the pen and paper icon). With two weeks available to make introductions and boot camp, a holiday break of up to two weeks occurs immediately prior to scrims starting and, only one week later, official games. Within a span of approximately eight weeks, the regular split will be finished and candidates for playoffs will be decided. Also note the relatively few days off and 'live' week in which the team is due to play on stage. The fast-paced and results-focussed environment created within a schedule like this is not vastly different from descriptions of high-performance sport (Eubank et al., 2014), and has been reported to influence the practices and experiences of coaches in esports (Watson et al., 2022).

In highlighting both the potential for almost year-long competition and multiple league seasons (splits) within it, it's also evident that teams may have little time for rest and recovery in the form of an offseason. In certain esports games, there is also a prominent 'grind culture' surrounding amateur and professional play, which may be somewhat propagated by the frequency and duration of official competition. Grind culture is generally characterised as players attempting to play 'as many games as frequently as possible' (Abbott et al., 2022, p. 1), and has been linked to instances of burnout, physical ailments, poor performance, and early career termination. In their investigation of perceived training effectiveness in League of Legends, Abbott et al. (2022) reported that players felt pressure to play a high volume of games, even during splits, in order to avoid their rank (or more specifically League Points or LP) 'decaying' as a result of playing less. Whilst some volume of games is necessary to maintain a sense of sharpness in terms of one's skills (mechanics), maintaining their publicly available rank was seen as important by

Table 7.1 Event, Route to Event, Duration of the Event

Event	Route to event (e.g., How long are the splits/tournaments/seasons for qualifying teams)	Duration of the event (e.g., how long could the winners be involved in)
2023 League of Legends World Championships	LCS (NA) 2 Splits (Spring & Summer) - Regular Season – 8 Weeks (18 games) - Playoffs (Top 6 Teams) – 4 Weeks (Minimum 9 games, maximum 25 games) LEC (EMEA) 3 Splits (Winter, Spring, Summer Splits) - Regular Season – 3 weeks, 9 games - Playoffs (Top 8 teams) – 3 Weeks (Minimum 10 games, maximum 21 games) Season Finals (Top 6) - 3 Weeks (Minimum 9 games, maximum 25 games) LPL (China) - 2 Splits (Spring & Summer) - Regular Season – 10 Weeks (16 Bo3 Games, minimum 32 games, maximum 48 games) - Playoffs (Top 10 teams) – 3 Weeks (9 games minimum, 35 games maximum) LCK (South Korea) - 2 Splits (Spring & Summer) - 9 Weeks (18 Bo3 games, 36 minimum, 54 maximum) - Playoffs – 2 Weeks (Minimum 9 games, maximum 25 games)	Worlds Qualifying Series - 4th Seed from LEC & LCS play in 1 × Bo5 to advance to Worlds Play-in stage Worlds Play-in Stage - 1 Week (minimum 5 games, maximum 15 games) Worlds Group Stage - 1 Week (minimum 6 games excluding tiebreakers). - Top 2 from each group advance to the knockout stage Worlds Knockout stage - 3 weeks (minimum 9 games, maximum 15 games)

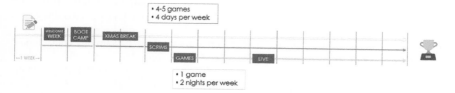

Figure 7.1 An example of the competitive schedule of a major ERL team in LoL.

players in order to prove their worth to current or future employers (i.e., teams). However, for a number of players, the grind was associated with negative physical and mental health consequences. Abbott et al. conclude that more should be done to encourage organisations to reduce the emphasis on rank as well as improve awareness of well-being, burnout, and more effective approaches to training (e.g., deliberate practice and use of goals).

7.5 Conclusion

In this chapter, we explored the different settings in which players compete, from online teams to on-stage tournaments, and discussed some of the advantages and challenges associated with them. In online teams, digital platforms such as Discord enable diverse teams to conjugate across competitive levels to train and compete, but may struggle to build a cohesive team due to a lack of non-verbal and informal communication. Teams that train together in-person have more opportunities to build team cohesion and close connections, but present alternative challenges such as less clear divisions between work and life/leisure, and professional challenges for the coach. This chapter finally concluded by highlighting the intensity of the competitive schedule in League of Legends and introducing the notion of grind culture, which appears to prevail across many games. Coaches, support staff and other decision makers involved with players are encouraged to consider strategies to avoid the potentially detrimental effects on players' performance, health, and well-being that result from a high volume of games with little rest.

References

Abbott, C., Watson, M., & Birch, P. (2022). Perceptions of effective training practices in league of legends: A qualitative exploration. *Journal of Electronic Gaming and Esports*, *1*(1), 1–11.

Arnold, R., & Sarkar, M. (2015). Preparing athletes and teams for the Olympic Games: Experiences and lessons learned from the world's best sport psychologists. *International Journal of Sport and Exercise Psychology, 13*(1), 4–20. https://doi.org/10.1080/1612197X.2014.932827

Cruickshank, A., & Collins, D. (2015). The sport coach. In I. O'Boyle, D. Murray, & P. Cummins (Eds.), *Leadership in sport* (pp. 155–172). https://doi.org/10.1017/CBO9781107415324.004

Esports Charts. (2022). *2022 World Championship [Worlds 2022]/Statistics*. Available at: https://escharts.com/tournaments/lol/2022-world-championship (Accessed: April 26, 2023)

Eubank, M., Nesti, M., & Cruickshank, A. (2014). Understanding high performance sport environments: Impact for the professional training and supervision of sport psychologists. *Sport and Exercise Psychology Review, 10*(2), 30–37.

Holt, N. L., & Strean, W. B. (2001). Reflecting on initiating sport psychology consultation: A self-narrative of neophyte practice. *The Sport Psychologist, 15*(2), 188–204.

Hurley, O. A. (2021). Sport cyberpsychology in action during the COVID-19 pandemic (opportunities, challenges, and future possibilities): A narrative review. *Frontiers in Psychology, 12*, 621283.

Lisk, T. C., Kaplancali, U. T., & Riggio, R. E. (2012). Leadership in multiplayer online gaming environments. *Simulation & Gaming, 43*(1), 133–149.

Pedraza-Ramirez, I., Mathorne, O., Ramaker, B., Watson, M., Laborde, S., & Raab, M. (2019). A case study of a high performance esports environment. In G. Amesberger, S. Würth, & T. Finkenzeller (Eds.) *51st Congress of the German Society of Sport Psychology* (p. 71). University of Salzburg. http://asp2020.at/fileadmin/user_upload/Abstractband_asp2020_Salzburg.pdf

Pereira, R., Wilwert, M. L., & Takase, E. (2016). Contributions of sport psychology to the competitive gaming: an experience report with a professional team of league of legends. *International Journal of Applied Psychology, 6*(2), 27–30.

Pilgrim, J., Kremer, P., & Robertson, S. (2018). The self-regulatory and task-specific strategies of elite-level amateur golfers in tournament preparation. *The Sport Psychologist, 32*(3), 169–177.

Thomson, K. E., & Trigwell, K. R. (2018). The role of informal conversations in developing university teaching? *Studies in Higher Education, 43*(9), 1536–1547.

Wagner, M. G. (2006, June). On the scientific relevance of eSports. In *International Conference on Internet Computing*, Las Vegas, Nevada (pp. 437–442).

Watson, M., Smith, D., Fenton, J., Pedraza-Ramirez, I., Laborde, S., & Cronin, C. (2022). Introducing esports coaching to sport coaching (not as sport coaching). *Sports Coaching Review*, 1–20.

8 Esports coaching and support

Matthew Watson and Kabir Bubna

8.1 Brief history of esports coaching

In 2002, journalist Richard Baimbridge wrote the following in an article for WIRED magazine: *"It's getting there. By most measures, videogaming is already a sport, and gamers are a highly evolved breed of extreme athlete. The top players form teams, compete in leagues, hire full-time coaches, and adopt strict training regimens."*

This is a fairly remarkable quote for a variety of reasons, not least the date of its authorship. We have already described how teams at the upper echelons of the esports industry increasingly resemble their counterparts in 'traditional' sports, particularly in terms of the staff in place around e'athletes (Watson et al., 2021). However, this shift towards professionalisation is typically described as a relatively recent evolution in esports. Certainly, it is uncommon now for a team competing in major game titles, such as League of Legends (LoL), Counter-Strike: Global Offensive (CS:GO), and Rocket League, to do so without at least one dedicated coach. The notion that esports teams had full-time coaches as early as 2002 may come as a surprise to many, and we may wonder why that is (Box 8.1).

In academic spheres, the scientific study of coaches (or about coaching) in esports has received very little attention (Watson et al., 2022). Even when broadening one's search terms to include video games, the act of coaching or role of a coach returns very little of relevance. In a 2009 paper titled "Collaboration and Learning in the Video Game Rock Band", published in the Proceedings of the Emerging Technologies Conference, there is mention of "In-game coaching" (p. 8) from fellow band members improving learning and enjoyment in the music video game Rock Band. Earlier still, in a 2007 Master's Degree piece on skill acquisition in gaming, Amanaborg describes how more experienced players would commonly coach less experienced ones in the game "Lineage". A more tentative link can be found in Belchior et al. (2013), who seem to have brought in an established coach to guide participants through the game Medal of Honor as part of their examination of the potential for the game to improve selective visual attention in older adults. Of course this is not an exploration of coaching, but perhaps suggests esports coaches weren't all that uncommon at the time.

DOI: 10.4324/9781003322382-8

Box 8.1   The first esports coach

It's hard to establish exactly who was the first to use the title of coach in esports, but it seems that whoever it was would have been involved in Starcraft in the early 2000s. For example, South Korean Starcraft player Lim "BoxeR" Yo-Hwan may have been coaching other players in some capacity as early as 2004. In 2008, former player Kim "Garimto" Dong Soo is reported to have taken on a formal coaching role with KTF MagicNs after returning from military service.

Perhaps the first academic scholars to actively involve coaches as participants in research were Kim and Thomas (2015), who interviewed two coaches and a number of players. Kim and Thomas were specifically exploring the career stages on the path to becoming a professional StarCraft player in South Korea, but at various points highlighted that coaches clearly held a position of significant decision-making power. Indeed, when entering the competitive environment, players needed to "rebuild their basic skills according to coaches' styles" (p. 181) and gain recognition from coaches in order to get the opportunity to play and receive feedback. Whilst struggling to be selected by the coach as one of the team delegates, one e'athlete spoke of being "afraid of being forgotten by my coach" (p. 181) and being jealous of friends that had more interactions with the coach. More recently, Himmelstein et al. (2017) mentioned the role of the coach in their discussion of techniques to achieve optimal performance, albeit briefly. Specifically, Himmelstein et al. mention that coaches should "utilize and train" (p. 14) both mental and mechanical skills. Thus, it seems that coaches were more-or-less established in practice, as a primary decision maker and in charge of the training of players, despite receiving scant attention in research.

Interestingly, in their systematic review of the cognitive and in-game performance factors in esports, Pedraza-Ramirez et al. (2020) highlight a number of points relevant for esports coaches specifically. For example, coaches should be aware that overly long sessions may incur a performance decline, coaches need to be mindful of players' psychological needs, and that coaches may benefit from education focussing on how to coach. The latter point is mentioned as a future challenge, ostensibly due to the lack of research on esports training and coaching practices.

8.2   The role of the esports coach

In his (2009) PhD dissertation, Taylor describes the behaviour of coaches he saw whilst attending the Major League Gaming 2008 Toronto Open Halo 3 tournament: "*During play, no one but the players, referees, security guards, press, and team 'coaches' – who stood or paced directly behind their team, motivating and coordinating team play – were allowed in the cordoned-off area*" (p. 30). Perhaps rather critically, he then goes on to surmise that the coaches' function "*is to take on the role of shouting map callouts for the entire team*" (p. 192). At the time of writing, there is very little academic, peer-reviewed work available to say whether these behaviours are typical for the role, nor indeed to build a robust description of the — esports coach's responsibilities and methods off-stage (i.e., outside of competition). A number of descriptions found in academic texts are listed in Table 8.1, although it should be noted that these descriptions were used to illustrate to readers what the role entails and were not based on empirical work in the studies themselves.

Of the few available empirical investigations into the role of the esports coach, Sabtan et al. (2022) interviewed four head LoL coaches, one analyst, and one general manager operating in North America or Europe. These six participants were each asked questions about performance assessment methods, training in esports, general game knowledge, and challenges faced by coaches in esports. Sabtan et al. reported that LoL coaches have a number of key objectives: to utilise and integrate players' and teams' strengths (particularly in relation to the game champions they play); to develop effective communication and trust between players; to identify weaknesses in a players' micro (technical) skill and provide training in this area; to analyse opponents' gameplay and co-create with players a relevant macro/strategy; to set weekly goals for players to help them improve; and to support players' motivation to practice. Whilst these objectives may sound intuitive, the small sample size of four coaches and limited demographic information (e.g., competitive level, years of experience) rather limits the generalisability of the findings. Equally, the objectives identified above align with a predominantly coach-led coaching approach, and it's likely that alternative coaching philosophies and methods exist. Indeed, Sabtan et al. go on to state that a head coach's role is

Table 8.1 Some Descriptions of the Role of the Esports Coach Found in Academic Articles

Authors	Definition of the Esports Coach
Difrancisco-Donoghue et al. (2019)	The head coach is the senior individual who trains the team and oversees, manages practices, and provides game-specific training for the team (p. 4).
Hedlund et al. (2020)	A game coach has a direct effect on the team's or player's actions in preparation for or while playing the game. These coaches analyse game play, tactics, and strategies; identify the team's, players', and opponents' strengths, weaknesses, and playing styles; and develop game plans and strategies for victory based on the team's or players' abilities, the score of the game, and the version of the game being used (p. 190).
Lipovaya et al. (2018)	During a match, it is expected that a coach of a CS:GO team will provide tactical support with his knowledge, review the team's mistakes, and help the team members with issues not related to the game itself. In R6 teams, the coach must study the adversary and the maps to formulate strategies for the team. In both games, the coach also has to perform some activities – such as motivating and leading the team – that are similar to the role of a captain (p. 10).

to determine "whatever the team needs in order to perform at peak performance" (p. 14), thus not all coaches will necessarily share the aforementioned objectives.

One area that appears to be common to the coaching role in a number of esports, particularly LoL, is scouting new players. In Box 8.2, professional LoL coach James 'Torok' Thomsen discusses some of the details of the scouting process from the coach's perspective. The themes of talent identification and development is further explored in Chapter 9.

Box 8.2   James 'Torok' Thomsen on scouting players

To give an accurate and concise summary of what may constitute an effective yet also generic process to identify the best possible player(s), it's vital to acknowledge some of the key axioms that affect the process. These are the available budget, goals of the team, dynamic of any retained players, personality factors, communication skills, game sense, and mechanical talent. Whilst this is far from an exhaustive list, these often form the basis for building an accurate player profile, which is the aim of a well-conducted scouting report and should be outlined at the beginning of a scouting process.

Following logically, it's then the delicate balancing act of all the desired traits that will lead to finding your ideal player(s). On one hand, you may compromise mechanical talent in a certain role in order to claim the benefits that a player may grant to game sense, communication skills, and diligence in practice. On the other, it's vital to ensure the team has at least one (if not more) player(s) who can reliably produce mechanical results inside of the game, regardless of other factors, as winning is a core aspect of any competitive team and you cannot win consistently competing beneath the skill level of the competition.

To provide a practical example, a player may be a great communicator with a glowing personality and game sense, but there's little use in having five of them in a team as their mechanical output is below the level necessary relative to the competition and every game you play will be fighting uphill against the very real deficit in the colloquial, yet aptly phrased "hands department."

How, then, can you begin to learn about these variables in the scouting process?

An initial tool that is extremely effective is obtaining "VODs" (videos on demand) from a player's perspective, which also captures their communication. Whilst I specialise in League of Legends, I can confidently say that "POV VODs" would be a great starting point in recruiting for any team-based competitive esports such as CS:GO, Valorant, or Rocket League.

When watched by a knowledgeable eye, POV VODs can give great indicators about the desirable elements of a player's performance and begin to add more granular details to the profiling process, whilst also being relatively time efficient. This is due to the fact that significant observable markers of a player's mechanical ability, as well as their in-game thought process, are visibly on display and often in a competitive situation. Specifically, you can see their "clicks", which may signal intent, as well as show how good they are at "spacing," (a micro skill that is regularly used in LoL) when performing under pressure. Furthermore, the VOD will show how effectively they utilise the in-game camera ("camera control"), which is how a player gathers information within the game outside of the minimap and team communication. All of these aspects would go under the umbrella of mechanical skill. However, VODs are also very useful for illuminating some elements of game sense that can't be observed in any other way, such as how the player in question is coordinating lane assignments with his team relative to the game state and deliberately waiting for the optimal moment in the game for them to join a team fight.

Other scouting techniques should also be utilised, however, as perhaps you (the coach) were sent cherry-picked VODs from a player or their agent that showcases them in their best light, however upon reaching out for references from past coaches and players, you discover a claim that they're widely inconsistent and even toxic. Thus, the utilisation of many sources of information will help paint an increasingly accurate picture of a given player and raise questions that would need answering should you decide to sign them.

Naturally, looking at data sources (such as freely available public websites) that show a player's competitive statistics or more in-depth, custom-built data analytics that can judge players neutrally whilst respecting the laws of double-blind, randomised clinical trials can once again provide more of an insight into what type of player you're looking at. Data is a precious tool when utilised effectively and with the context in mind. No decision should ever be solely based on data whilst scouting, but it has an important place in guiding the coach in the right direction towards potential players, affirming other observed strengths and weaknesses and making the call on difficult decisions.

As a final note, holistic discussions with the player about the game, themselves and more general topics can be a great way to gather further information as to whether they may be the right fit for your project. As in any other team sport, the human element is invaluable and therefore making sure you select players with both the character and competitive skillset to fit your context is vital in ensuring you're able to make an informed and optimal decision.

In summary, the scouting process for esports coaches involves gathering accurate information from as varied and diverse sources as possible in order to be able to draw correct conclusions and precisely profile a player. In doing so effectively, thousands of potential candidates are reduced to just the best few players, whom you can then bring forward to trial. Scouting will be continuously refined over time as private or public actors (e.g., academic researchers) uncover new insights and methods to enhance the recruitment process.

Overall, given the lack of academic study on the role of the esports coach, it's difficult to provide a precise description of the role and associated responsibilities. Whilst there are numerous anecdotal accounts that suggest some common functions (e.g., to analyse gameplay and develop game plans), there's likely to be significant variation in the responsibilities of coaches in esports as a result of the demands/ rules of different games (e.g., can training exercises be created, can coaches talk to players during competition), the specific needs of the players with whom they work and expectations of their organisation or institution. This is not dissimilar to coaching in sport except that sport coaching has clearer distinctions between different sporting contexts (e.g., recreational, developmental, or performance settings) and stages of development that determine the primary responsibilities of coaches. Simply applying these same criteria to esports is difficult for a host of reasons. For example, video games are designed to be the perfect coach when initially developing game-specific skills and expertise; they provide constant feedback, opportunities for mastery, and optimal challenge (Gee, 2005). Thus, at a grassroots or recreational level of esports, a coach's role likely requires a more holistic approach (e.g., individual and group preparation, interpersonal skills) than a sport coach working with players at a comparable stage of development. More research is certainly necessary to determine the essential functions of esports coaches.

8.3 Necessary knowledge and skills for an esports coach

In the absence of a precise definition of the responsibilities of esports coaches, it's perhaps more useful to consider the knowledge and skills that esports coaches require to perform their role. One common question is whether coaches require a high level of skill or prior playing experience in their respective games. Certainly, the transition from athlete to coach is a common route individuals take in both traditional sports and esports. At the time of writing, six of the ten head coaches of the LoL European Championship (LEC) were previously professional players in major regional leagues or higher. Is high-level playing experience therefore an advantage for coaches albeit not essential? And how is it beneficial if so? Game knowledge, first-hand familiarity with the demands on players, and social/cultural capital to open the right career doors could all be relevant factors here. For potential employers, a clearer understanding of the factors that contribute to a successful career transition from player to coach, as well as the key competencies of coaches, is important to appoint the right individual.

8.3.1 The pros of being an ex-player

As mentioned above, for a former professional player, the social and cultural capital accrued through a successful playing career may help them to find a coaching position following the cessation of their playing career. This is not uncommon in sport and has been described as 'fast-tracking', whereby elite athletes benefit from special concessions in order to accelerate their progression into high-performance coaching positions (Rynne, 2014). The assumption is that former players are familiar with the professional environment, high-level gameplay, and the process of coaching such that they will be able to reproduce it themselves. Ostensibly, a former professional player is likely to have amassed sufficient time playing a game to possess a high-level of expertise and relevant tacit knowledge (i.e., processes and techniques learned by the everyday experiences of doing them). Given the limited coach education pathways in esports at present (Watson et al., 2022), relying on this assumed knowledge is certainly understandable from the perspective of an employer. There have also been several high-profile examples of the player to coach transition. For example, the case of Bjergsen, who retired as the professional mid-laner for Team Solo Mid (TSM) in the North America League of Legends Championship Series in 2020 and assumed the role of the head coach within the same organisation. This added to his credibility and seemingly made the process of establishing buy-in from players smoother, providing Bjergsen with a degree of confidence that allowed him to perform at his best within the new role. Due to his lengthy tenure as a player, Bjergsen's knowledge of the nuances of the mechanics and strategies within the game would also be vast.

8.3.2 The cons of being an ex-player

In some cases, the fast-tracking of a former professional player into a high-performance coaching position may have its downsides. For example, whilst knowledge of the game itself and tacit knowledge of being in the team environment may help with building rapport and provide an initial source of confidence, much of this knowledge is likely to be grounded in intuition and instinct. Without supplementary coaching skills, these individuals ("intuitive experts"; Nash & Collins, p. 467) would not be the most effective at developing players as they will struggle to explain their decision-making processes. More specifically, professional players have practised to the point that their performances require little attention to the steps or processes by which an action was planned or carried out. As a result of this 'expert-induced amnesia' (Beilock & Carr, 2001, p. 703), former professional (expert) players may find it difficult to articulate tactics or the execution of skills. This challenge may be heightened by the frequent game updates in esports. If a coach is unable to explain the processes behind a decision, then helping players to learn to make appropriate decisions when faced with a new meta, champion/hero/agent or map (that is unfamiliar to the coach) is all the more difficult.

Another challenge for the former professional player as they begin coaching is that, whilst the social and cultural capital associated with being a former pro player can help with building rapport and finding common ground with players, the nature of the relationship between coach and player is different than between peers/players. A novice coach, such as a former professional player that has been fast-tracked into a position without any form of coach education, is likely to engage in a suboptimal process of trial and error to navigate the power dynamic between themselves and their players (Nash & Collins, 2006). In this instance, coaches may fall back on how they themselves were coached – an occurrence that is not uncommon in coaches generally (Nordmann, 2006) – yet given the relative youth of esports coaching in comparison to sport and lack of coach education to date (Watson et al., 2022), their coaches may have been engaged in a process of trial and error themselves.

In considering the pros and cons above, we are not stating that a former professional player in a particular esports cannot be a good coach. Rather, we are suggesting that the process of transitioning from a professional player into the role of a coach is not a straightforward nor unproblematic process, especially when this is fast-tracked without any formal coach education. On the other hand, we are also suggesting that an esports coach does not necessarily need to have been a professional player competing at a high level in order to be effective. This would seem to be uncontroversial when considering the general responsibilities of an esports coach, such as organising practice sessions, developing tactics and strategy, and guiding a player or team throughout the competitive period. To do this effectively, coaches must use a *variety* of different types of knowledge beyond knowledge of a particular game. For example, within their integrative definition of coaching effectiveness, Côté and Gilbert (2009) describe three areas of knowledge that coaches need in order to be effective. These three areas are known as the triad of knowledge and include professional knowledge, interpersonal knowledge, and intrapersonal knowledge (see Table 8.2).

8.3.3 Professional knowledge

Professional knowledge refers to the knowledge coaches attain as they understand the nuances of their context. Many coaches will have at some point been an active player within their context, which helps develop their knowledge relating to the games mechanics and interactions, and can aid their ability to provide feedback to players in the future. Furthermore, coaches who have a dearth of coaching experience can reflect on their experiences to better understand how to tackle certain situations in their current context such as planning training sessions.

8.3.4 Interpersonal knowledge

Interpersonal knowledge reflects a coach's ability to effectively communicate with their team. A large part of effective coaching relies on the ability for the coach to convey their feedback/message in a way that is digestible to their players; therefore, it is important for the coach to understand the different ways the players are

Table 8.2 The Three Knowledge Areas and Examples as Provided by Côté and Gilbert (2009)

Knowledge Area	Example of Subject Matters
Professional Knowledge	Knowledge of the game (mechanics & strategies) Knowledge of athlete requirements Pedagogical skill Coaching experience Playing experience
Interpersonal Knowledge	Social Contexts Relationships/Impression Management
Intrapersonal Knowledge	Coaching Philosophy and Values Emotional Intelligence Self-regulation

receptive to feedback. On top of this, it is important for coaches to not only manage the coach–athlete relationship (see also Chapter 6), but also act as a mediator for player–player relationship to effectively settle any conflict and promote the development of social cohesion.

8.3.5 Intrapersonal knowledge

Intrapersonal knowledge looks inwards to the coach. It uncovers their own coaching philosophy and values, and urges coaches to engage in reflective practices to better understand themselves and their impact on the developmental landscape of individuals/the team. Coaches should also be aware of their boundaries so that they can regulate their behaviour and provide a consistent image to the players to ensure that respect, trust, and buy-in to the team environment can be cultivated.

One of the common responsibilities described in academic and anecdotal articles on esports coaching is the need to set the vision or overall goal for the team. This is also a common function of sports coaches, although it seems that the duration of this vision in esports is somewhat shorter, perhaps one year or less, due to the shorter-term contracts and higher turnover of e'athletes and staff in esports (LeNorgant, 2019). A practising esports coach looking to develop their knowledge of creating a vision may be interested in the body of work in sport on nested planning (Abraham & Collins, 2011), which typically encompasses an overarching, longer-term goal (e.g., one year; macro level) broken down into smaller month-to-month or week-to-week goals (meso level) and day-to-day goals (micro level). When coaches engage in 'nested thinking' they align each type of goal with one another so that each goal serves a purpose towards the future development of individuals and the team (see Figure 8.1).

8.3.6 Macro goals

Macro goals are the largest goals and the overarching goals that will guide the team throughout the season. These goals should identify appropriate aims and objectives that the team should look to achieve. Using Figure 8.1, a type of macro goal would be to qualify for the end of year international competition (Worlds). Using a team within the LEC in LoL as an example, many would aim to represent their region at this prestigious event to match-up against the best teams across the globe. By identifying the overall aim of the team, it makes it clearer for the coach to set expectations towards the e'athletes and provides a clear and consistent target that the team works towards.

8.3.7 Meso goals

These goals are intermediate in length, usually spanning over one to three months. These goals effectively break down the macro goal into smaller digestible chunks, providing teams with direction as their season evolves and moulds. At this level, coaches should aim to incorporate and identify the tactical vision of the team as this stage affords enough time for tactical development to be evidenced.

Goal	Objectives	Timeline & Activity		
Macro	• Qualify for international competition. • Rank within the top 3 of the domestic region • Make it out of group stages at international events	Season 1	Season 2	Season 3
Meso	• Develop levels of group cohesiveness • Establish preferred playstyles and team philosophy • Make it to the finals of domestic competition	Winter Split • Induction to teams' values and philosophy creation • Recurring team bonding / social activities	Spring Split	Summer Split
Micro	• Develop a drafting identity • Maintain a positive team environment	Daily/ Weekly • Engage in theory crafting with the team • Implement positive scrim practice initiatives		

Figure 8.1 An example of nested planning for an LEC League of Legends team.

8.3.8 *Micro goals*

Micro goals focus on understanding the day-to-day/weekly operations of the team. At this level, coaches should identify what technical development is necessary for the team as they prepare for competition. Additionally, coaches are required to be flexible and adjust practices or respond to potential conflicts as they arise or handle injuries or illnesses of their e'athletes (Box 8.3).

8.4 Esports coach development

Recognising the lack of research into the role of the esports coach, Watson et al. (2022) sought to explore the careers and practices of esports coaches and the

Box 8.3   An example of nested planning in Rocket League by Coach James 'Jimmah' Forshaw

As esports coaches, we are afforded a unique level of freedom in our practice. We are presented with a team, an organisation, a competitive league and the, often essential, goal to win. Whilst this freedom offers us an open landscape to practise coaching in a way we find desirable, we are presented with challenges that are unique to the industry of esports. Many of these challenges emerge from the problem of team planning and programming. Without institutional or organisational guidelines, predetermined content, reporting, and conduct, coaches can adopt a variety of resources, frameworks, assessments, and reporting tools to assist their practice at their discretion.

In solving the problem of planning and programming for my Rocket League team, my practices are coloured by my experiences as an educator. Many of the approaches, frameworks, and resources that inform my practice as an educator share some continuity and alignment with my coaching. One of these methods is planning and programming through a *scope and sequence*, which in education is predicated upon the framework of content and delivery of a program. The *scope* refers to the content and goals that a program aims to deliver and cover. The *sequence* refers to the order and progression that the content is delivered and how goals will be achieved.

Within the landscape of competitive Rocket League, this involves identifying where a program is applicable, often bound to a set time, such as a preseason or a period of time set between competitions. Goals can be generated through formative data, which can include replay analysis, observational notes, and player interviews. These goals can inform the kinds of preparation the players will undertake, which becomes the content of the program. By setting explicit goals and outcomes, along with a plan of how players will work towards these goals and outcomes, creates the foundation for a successful scope and sequence.

experiences that shape them. In the study, 14 head coaches from third-tier (n = 1), second-tier (n = 12), or first-tier (n = 1) LoL teams across three regions, Europe, North America, and Oceania, were interviewed as part of the study. Watson et al. reported four themes following their thematic analysis that overall emphasised a lack of structure, support, and stability around coaches' careers that impacted their practice and well-being. More specifically, in the absence of formal coach education, coaches' learning was largely experiential and career progression somewhat relied on coaches' social networks rather than demonstrable training or qualifications. Perhaps as a result, and in combination with the short competitive seasons, coaches felt the pressure to produce results, which in turn led to more negative emotional experiences and seemed to increase the use of more coach-led approaches. Finally, the findings of Watson et al. highlight how coaching in esports involves some fundamental differences to coaching in sport. For example, frequent game updates in LoL pushed coaches to scout other global regions that had earlier access to updates in order to accelerate their understanding of changes and current strategy.

Overall, the findings of Watson et al. (2022) point towards a need for coach education within esports that supports the more holistic, interpersonal, and intrapersonal aspects of coaching, and indicates that a desire exists amongst coaches for a more structured career path. This echoes the conclusion of an earlier systematic review paper by Pedraza-Ramirez et al. (2020) who called for education for coaches focussing on the process of coaching, for example, through esports coaching courses as well as developmental positions within academy teams. The emphasis on the need to support esports coaches in more holistic knowledge areas is also evident in a qualitative study by Poulus et al. (2022), in which professional LoL, Rainbow Six: Siege and CS:GO players perceived their coaches as "being less holistic in their coaching skillset; they were more likely to be a specialist in a specific role" (p. 751).

In recognition of the aforementioned research, the International Federation of Esports Coaches – a not-for-profit organisation dedicated to the professional development of coaches in esports – established the first structured certification pathway for esports coaches. At the time of writing, the first two levels of the pathway are delivered online and asynchronously and feature modules on sport psychology (e.g., motivation and confidence), pedagogy (e.g., planning and delivery coaching sessions), and other aspects of professional practice (e.g., safeguarding and working with parents). Further levels will aim to contextualise knowledge and encourage application to coaches' own contexts via more interactive and synchronous activity. However, contemporary sports coaching literature describes how coaches learn from a range of sources, including formal (e.g., courses), non-formal, and informal education; hence, research is warranted into areas such as coach mentorship and communities of practice in esports.

8.5 Conclusion

This chapter outlines and explores the skills and competencies needed to effectively assume a coaching role. However, due to the current volatility of the esports industry, there appears to be a lack of consistency in coaching standards which could highlight the need for formal coach education similar to those offered for coaches in traditional contexts. By developing and garnering interaction in such types of opportunities, a baseline standard to coaching can be evidenced, providing organisations with well-equipped staff, and consequently providing professional developmental opportunities for those who seek it.

References

Abraham, A., & Collins, D. (2011). Taking the next step: Ways forward for coaching science. *Quest, 63*(4), 366–384.

Beilock, S. L., & Carr, T. H. (2001). On the fragility of skilled performance: What governs choking under pressure? *Journal of Experimental Psychology: General, 130*(4), 701.

Belchior, P., Mariske, M., Sisco, S. M., Yam, A., Bavelier, D., Ball, K., & Mann, W. C. (2013). Video game training to improve selective visual attention in older adults. *Computers and Human Behavior, 29*, 1318–1324.

Côté, J., & Gilbert, W. (2009). An integrative definition of coaching effectiveness and expertise. *International Journal of Sports Science & Coaching, 4*(3), 307–323.

Difrancisco-Donoghue, J., Balentine, J., Schmidt, G., & Zwibel, H. (2019). Managing the health of the eSport athlete: An integrated health management model. *BMJ Open Sport and Exercise Medicine, 5*(1), 1–6.

Gee, J. P. (2005). Learning by design: Good video games as learning machines. *E-Learning and Digital Media, 2*(1), 5–16. https://doi.org/10.2304/elea.2005.2.1.5

Hedlund, D., Fried, G., & Smith, R. (2020). *Esports business management*. Champaign, IL: Human Kinetics.

Himmelstein, D., Liu, Y., & Shapiro, J. L. (2017). An exploration of mental skills among competitive league of legend players. *International Journal of Gaming and Computer-Mediated Simulations, 9*(2), 1–21.

Kim, S. H., & Thomas, M. K. (2015). A stage theory model of professional video game players in South Korea: The socio-cultural dimensions of the development of expertise. *Asian Journal of Information Technology, 14*(5), 176–186.

LeNorgant, E. J. (2019*). Sport-related anxiety and self-talk between traditional sports and esports*. Doctoral dissertation, California State University, Fresno.

Lipovaya, V., Lima, Y., Grillo, P., Barbosa, C. E., De Souza, J. M., & Duarte, F. J. D. C. M. (2018). Coordination, communication, and competition in eSports: A comparative analysis of teams in two action games. In *Proceedings of 16th European Conference on Computer-Supported Cooperative Work-Exploratory Papers*. European Society for Socially Embedded Technologies (EUSSET).

Nash, C., & Collins, D. (2006). Tacit knowledge in expert coaching: Science or art? *Quest, 58*(4), 465–477. https://doi.org/10.1080/00336297.2006.10491894

Nordmann, L. (2006). A fresh approach to coach education. *Modern Athlete & Coach, 43*(3), 37–38.

Pedraza-Ramirez, I., Musculus, L., Raab, M., & Laborde, S. (2020). Setting the scientific stage for esports psychology: a systematic review. *International Review of Sport and Exercise Psychology, 13*(1), 319–352.

Poulus, D. R., Coulter, T. J., Trotter, M. G., & Polman, R. (2022). A qualitative analysis of the perceived determinants of success in elite esports athletes. *Journal of Sports Sciences, 40*(7), 742–753. https://doi.org/10.1080/02640414.2021.2015916

Rynne, S. (2014). 'Fast track' and 'traditional path' coaches: Affordances, agency and social capital. *Sport, Education and Society, 19*, 299–313. https://doi.org/10.1080/13573322.2012.670113

Sabtan, B., Cao, S., & Paul, N. (2022). Current practice and challenges in coaching esports players: An interview study with League of Legends professional team coaches. *Entertainment Computing, 42*, 100481.

Taylor, N. T. (2009). *Digital gaming goes pro*. Doctoral dissertation, York University, Toronto.

Watson, M., Abbott, C., & Pedraza-Ramirez, I. (2021). A parallel approach to performance and sport psychology work in esports teams. *International Journal of Esports, 1*(1), 1–6.

Watson, M., Smith, D., Fenton, J., Pedraza-Ramirez, I., Laborde, S., & Cronin, C. (2022). Introducing esports coaching to sport coaching (not as sport coaching). *Sports Coaching Review, 00*(00), 1–20. https://doi.org/10.1080/21640629.2022.2123960

9 Talent identification and development

Kabir Bubna and Remco Polman

9.1 What do we think of as talent in esports?

The development of expertise and what constitutes talent has been a controversial topic across multiple domains like music, art, science, and sport. There have been heated discussions whether expertise and talent are due to nature (your genetic or biological make-up) or nurture (your environment). The layman view (or those provided by many sports commentators and coaches) often prefers the nature view. They attribute exceptional skilled performance to inborn qualities, a God-given gift, which are unlikely to be modified by training or practice. These exceptional performers are viewed as having innate abilities, like superior reaction time, or timing which make them particularly suitable for the sport they participate in. However, from the literature it is clear that most traditional athletes do not have a systematically superior hardware system but outperform less skilled athletes because they have invested more in systematic training and/or have developed a superior knowledge base of their chosen sport.

Interestingly expertise differences in sport have not been a major topic of academic research until the late 1960s. Early work examined mainly pattern-recognition and knowledge across cognitive tasks. For example, Chase and Simon (1973) established that superior performance in chess players was due to enhanced pattern-based retrieval following years of practice and experience in chess. Similar results were found in other domains like physics. Importantly, superior performance is domain specific. For example, in several studies it has been found that expert performers are only able to come-up with faster and more accurate recognition for patterns in their chosen domain.

Although there has been little research in esports to date on the factors associated with expert performance, it is not unlikely that domain-specific pattern recognition is important. Through the process of practice and competition, e'athletes build-up domain-specific patterns in their long-term memory. We would argue that elite level e'athletes are more likely to use this stored information to discriminate and make comparisons between patterns they observe on the computer screen and those stored in memory. Cognitive psychology suggests that the recognition of complex displays as a pattern speeds up (you can make

DOI: 10.4324/9781003322382-9

quicker decisions) and enhances (deeper level) information processing (Craik & Lockhart, 1972). In addition, this augmented information in long-term memory enhances the ability of the e'athlete to reason, plan, and evaluate consequences of their actions (e.g., Ericsson & Lehmann, 1996). This would be supported by findings of Sorman et al. (2022) in a sample of DOTA e'athletes. This study showed that Medal and ranking was associated with performance on the Iowa Gambling Task (IGT) a measure of decision making under ambiguity. We believe that expert e'athletes are more forward looking and will assess existing alternatives more fully yet more quickly.

There is some preliminary evidence that there are greater adaptations in the brain of expert e'athletes compared to less skilled e'athletes. Hyun et al. (2013) found in a study involving 23 StarCraft pro-gamers that career length was associated with larger cortical volume in the parietal and frontal cortex and precentral gyrus. Interestingly, more wins in the Korea StarCraft Pro League was associated with the right superior frontal gyrus (r = .51) whereas a longer career resulted in faster completion and less errors on the Wisconsin Card Sorting Test (WCST). The latter is a test for assessing an individual's set-shifting capability (cognitive flexibility). Although interesting findings, there was no matched control group and the WCST is more a test to be used with patients with brain damage. Similarly, Tanaka et al. (2013) found a larger grey matter volume in Guilty Gear experts compared to a control group. The larger volume was associated with performance on the visual WM task. The latter was attributed to the nature of esports, requiring the ability to identify and memorise multiple objects in displays.

The difficulty with assessment of brain structures and performance on neuropsychological tests is that it is difficult to establish cause and effect. Hence, did the e'athlete get attracted to a particular esports because of their brain structure or did the engagement in esports change the brain structure? In addition, how relevant are the neuropsychological test to actual game performance.

Talent can be defined as an individual's ability or potential to supersede the average population in a particular field that requires training and specialised skills (Den Hartigh et al., 2018). In esports, most titles measure the skill mastery of their e'athletes base by using a ranking system that distributes players into different tiers (see Chapter 1). For instance, LoL has nine different rank classifications from Iron (lowest) to Challenger (highest). Other games will feature their own ranking system but will be based on a very similar algorithms that is now common across esports. Figure 9.1 further depicts the rank distribution among player bases in popular esports titles LoL and Valorant.

This ranking system is vital to the esports industry as it provides a baseline for competition at the amateur level, where tournaments are usually open entry for teams and the only regulation is for the team to average a certain rank. At the professional levels of participation, leagues may have specific rank requirements set out for their e'athletes and teams, this is very common in professional LoL (refer to Table 9.1).

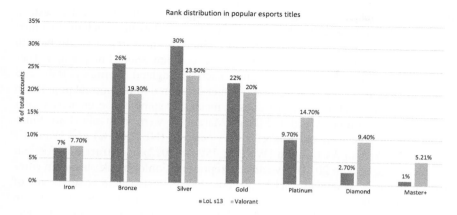

Figure 9.1 Comparison of Rank Distribution in LoL (Season 13) and Valorant. Adapted from Conroy et al. (2021) which shows the rank distribution in esports titles LoL, Dota 2, and Overwatch.

Table 9.1 Minimum Rank Requirements for Professional LoL

League	Region	Minimum Rank
LoL European Championship	Europe	Diamond 3
LoL Championship Series	North America	Diamond 1
European Regional League	Europe	Diamond 3

9.2 Talent identification and development

The two distinct fields known as talent identification (TID) and talent development (TDE) have helped coaches and organisations find, develop, and bring forth world-class talent to traditional sports. TID as described by Baker et al. (2012) understands the processes and techniques that may be used to 'spot' athletes who have the potential to excel at a high level, whereas TDE focusses on the techniques used to foster the wholistic development of an athlete that may have been identified previously (Abbott & Collins, 2004). The discussion around TID and TDE is also influenced by the nature versus nurture debate (Baker et al., 2012), as well as embracing additional factors (i.e., quality of training experience; Ericsson et al., 1993). Although both TID and TDE inform each other about developing elite athletes, they are often conducted in isolation.

In traditional sporting contexts (i.e., football, basketball, and rugby), TID has usually been conducted through practice/game observation by coaches and scouts (Roberts et al., 2019). This approach is problematic and ineffective as it does not rely on scientific and empirical evidences, but rather, a subjective view of what the observer determines to be an ideal athlete (Meylan et al., 2010). The biopsychosocial perspective perceives TID as complex in which athletes are evaluated by 'standard' sets of variables such as anthropometric and physical measures (i.e., weight, height, speed; e Silva et al., 2010) as well as their technical/tactical ability (Thomas et al., 2009). Despite more objective measures, it is still hard to predict who will make it at the professional level in any sport. For example, soccer players from four European leagues, such as England, Germany, Italy, and Spain, have been found to be taller and leaner compared to the normal population (Bloomfield et al., 2005), but that doesn't mean that some of the greatest soccer players, such as Lionel Messi and Diego Maradona, were relatively short. Similarly, although the National Basketball Association (NBA; 72%) and Women's National Basketball Association (WNBA; 75% in 2022) and American Football League (AFL; 56% in 2022) have an overrepresentation of black players in comparison to the US population (12.1%), this doesn't mean there is some sort of sport gene. This is a complex issue in which cultural differences also play an important role. Hence, why are black athletes underrepresented in sports like ice-hockey, speed skating, and swimming? Factors like societal expectations, familial or ethnic traditions, opportunity, and self-image are likely to interact with genetic attributes.

As esports does only require performance to be conducted through limited physical motor skills, it would be important to understand the technical, tactical, and cognitive skills needed by e'athletes to participate within high-performance contexts. To date, however, our understanding on this is still limited. For example, information processing is likely to be an important factor for many esports. There has been some discussion that aspects of information processing like response speed, working memory, and general intelligence are heritable. However, to date, objective tests assessing cognitive or perceptual abilities do not discriminate between levels of expertise for many domains. It is more likely that experts through their training can circumvent limitations of their hardware (e.g., reaction time).

TDE, on the other hand, focusses on creating training programmes to develop, nurture, and refine the skills of those identified as talented with the aim of building individuals that will bring success in future competitions. As identified above, due to its complex, non-linear, and dynamic nature (Abbott et al., 2005; Henriksen & Stambulova, 2017), a great challenge for any sporting organisation is to predict which talents identified in the TID process can fulfil their potential and beyond (Dimundo et al., 2022). In addition, because esports is still relatively young in its inception, the development of the most appropriate training and developmental strategies to nurture talent has not been identified.

9.3 Approaches to identifying and developing talent in esports

As the industry of professional esports continues to grow, organisations are always proactive in their roster development. This chapter will use LoL as a running example when further discussing the implementation of TID and TDE approaches. A qualitative study conducted by Meng-Lewis et al. (2022) to understand the dynamics of a career within esports briefly reported on the approaches that organisations may use when trying to identify talent. There are currently three main channels used by professional organisations: (a) reaching upper echelons of solo queue ranking, (b) references or recommendations by trusted industry professionals, and (c) competitive experience.

9.3.1 Reaching upper echelons of solo queue

As mentioned previously, competitive esports have a global ranking system. This system allows comparisons to be drawn between players with higher and lower rankings (Sanz-Matesanz et al., 2023). Looking at some of the rules that professional teams must adhere to (refer to Table 9.1), it comes as no surprise that coaches, managers, and other key stakeholders within the TID decision-making process will add weight towards the peak and current rank achieved by prospective e'athletes. A limitation of such a strategy is that only assess current potential and not future potential. In addition, the key determinant for esports success identified in the scoping review by Sanz-Matesanz et al. (2023) are teamwork and cooperation skills rather than personal statistics. As discussed in Chapter 6, team cohesion is more important than the rankings of each individual in a team.

9.3.2 Trusted industry referrals

As the world of esports is mainly located online, with amateur and semi-professional teams operating remotely, there is a large scope to effectively use social media to scout for talented individuals through the use of websites like Reddit or Twitter. Furthermore, Discord is a software which allows forums to be built for networking purposes between coaches, e'athletes, and teams (Freeman & Wohn, 2019). Individuals will use these pipelines to create looking-for team (LFT) posts. LFTs are akin to a CV one might use when applying for jobs, and will briefly describe competitive experience and accomplishments, aspirations, and preferred playstyles, and will also feature information about referees. In an industry where there is a possibility to never physically meet prospective e'athletes, these references can aid in the talent identification process as referees can provide additional information about the general attitude of the player and insights into the player's personality and adapt to the team culture of a particular organisation.

9.3.3 Previous competitive experience

Like traditional sporting environments, there is always a risk associated with accommodating an unproven rookie to any roster, therefore, to access the highest level of participation within esports, e'athletes usually build their competitive experiences through a myriad of events offered to hone their skills. Open entry tournaments are a good starting point for aspiring professionals, and current professional coaches may be watching these events for individuals with the calibre for further participation. European Regional Leagues (ERLs) and the development of the collegiate scene in North America are other avenues offered for aspiring professionals to consistently engage with competition and adhere to a training schedule. All these activities can be seen as scouting grounds with opportunities for progression depending on circumstance.

9.3.4 Developmental activities

Talent development is still underdeveloped in esports. Predominantly, players' practice routines through engagement in solo queues and scrims (Sabtan et al., 2022). Scrims are an organised environment where e'athletes will practise against another competitive teams that can be within the same level of competition or in another league. Teams can play anywhere between three and six games, with a break in between each game to review their strategy. Other avenues for practice afforded to teams is organising 1v1s or 2v2s with other e'athletes to practise specific fundamentals (i.e., lane matchups, specific champion interactions) or even utilising practice tool in isolation to refine combinations or test build pathways. In recent years, Riot Games have introduced 'Champions Queue' to LoL. Piloted on the North American servers, and then introduced to the European servers, champions queue combines features of solo queue (match-making system and temporary teams) and scrims (organised 5v5s with the communication) to allow another practice environment for high-ranking players and professionals.

Another faucet used for talent development that is common in esports like LoL is boot camping. Boot camping refers to the practice of travelling to another region, commonly South Korea usually during off-season periods (i.e., pre-season or in-between splits). During this time, e'athletes will spend most of their time trying to climb the solo queue ladder of the Korean server. Teams tend to gravitate to this server because as a region South Korea is considered one of the most successful esports regions, thus providing an opportunity for other e'athletes to compete in a notoriously competitive environment (Conroy et al., 2021).

Lastly, another prominent feature that is more common in esports is the wide range of educational material posted (i.e., guides and gameplay) on YouTube which e'athletes can use to gain knowledge about key concepts to develop their knowledge and skills. Furthermore, e'athletes can watch professional teams compete but also watch individual professional e'athletes' games as most of them will stream on Twitch, allowing for a portion of learning to be conducted socially (Abbott et al., 2022).

9.4 How effective have they been?

As indicated previously, there is at present little empirical and objective research on the efficacy of current TID practices. E'athletes face a high rate of turnover across rosters (LeNorgant, 2019), and professional career lengths are highly variable. The stars of esports can have successful careers that span over multiple years, whereas the lesser fortunate can be axed after only a few competitions. Furthermore, in the current state of the industry across various esports titles, there is a bit of a talent merry-go-round as e'athletes who may get released from one roster can be swiftly picked up by a rivalling or organisation of equal footing due to their built experience of competition. Even though there are opportunities for esports to hold scouting combines similar to those seen in the NBA and NFL, there is still an overall reluctance to sign rookie talents, with many organisations favouring to stick with the tried and tested.

When discussing talent development processes, recent academic research has started to investigate their effectiveness. Sabtan et al. (2022) showed that one of the biggest challenges in esports talent development was associated with the practice routines. Scrims are a focal point for the development of teams, and at the most professional levels, those scrim sessions can last up to six hours a day, which is also usually paired with additional individual practice (i.e., solo queue, review, 1v1s), making it common for players to practice around 10–12 hours each day. A study conducted by Pluss et al. (2022) investigating practice quantity discovered that over a 10-year period, e'athletes will spend around 16,000+ hours in practice. Prolonged engagement within this environment can have detrimental impact on an individual's physical and mental health (DiFrancisco-Donoghue et al., 2019). In addition, this volume of practice seems to be rather high compared to other domains. For example, Ericsson et al. (2007) has argued that 10 years or 10,000 hours of deliberate practice is associated with expert performance in many domains. Although there is significant variation in how many hours individuals practise to become an expert this is most likely to be an overestimation. In addition, practice only predicts up to 25% of the variance in chess, music, and sport (Macnamara et al., 2016), and there are likely other factors at work, including motivation and genetics, which determine performance. It seems that the excessive hours point to inefficiencies in the practice regimes of e'athletes. These excessive hours also have negative lifestyle outcomes and can result in burnout and subsequent dropout from esports altogether (Salo, 2021). Further research investigating practice effectiveness in LoL by Abbott et al. (2022) further highlights the consensus from esports athletes that the current provisions are perceived to be ineffective and rely heavily on the grind (high quantity) mindset.

Another issue that occurs during scrims is because of their length, players can lose focus which ultimately reduces the quality of practice as they might make decisions that are not natural to their usual performance behaviours. They might also purposefully play different playstyles to hide specific strategies from opponents, which can make the translation of performance from a practice environment to officials/stage harder. Such strategies are also against neural theories of learning. In particular, practice should as closely as possible resemble competitive situations to get maximum transfer (specificity of learning principle) (see Sigmundsson et al., 2017).

9.5 Talent transfer in esports

To enhance the probability to identify, choose, and develop talent, many sporting organisations across the world have developed talent transfer programs

(Collins et al., 2014). The aim of such programs (e.g., Pitch2Podium; Girls4Gold) is to identify already successful and skilled athletes in one particular sport and transfer them to another sport in which they have the potential to be successful at the elite level (MacNamara & Collins, 2015). There are examples of athletes switching successfully between rowing and cycling and athletics and skeleton.

Currently, there have been no scientific studies on talent transfer in esports. However, the similarities between first-person shooting games make this an area in which this is likely to be possible. An example of this talent transfer is e-athletes participating in battle royale esports. Games like PUBG, Fortnite, and Call of Duty Warzone allow players to take skills developed in one game and reapply them within a different context successfully. If anything, such transfer is most likely to be successful when completed during the adolescent years. To this end Hayman et al. (2021) have proposed a model which can be applied to the esports context. The adolescent Sport Talent Transfer model is presented in Figure 9.2 and consists of four stages. In the first stage the e'athletes realise that despite early success they are not going to succeed in their selected esports. Because the e'athletes' life goal is to be a professional e'athlete irrespective of the genre, they will be susceptible to transfer to another esports. In the next phase, the e'athletes adapt to the demands of the newly selected esports. Because they already have a good level of the required skills, they will experience early success with relatively little effort. Success breeds success and the e'athletes will be more motivated to improve their skill and increase their training load to meet their lifegoal. In the final stages, the e'athlete changes their alliance and develops a new identity.

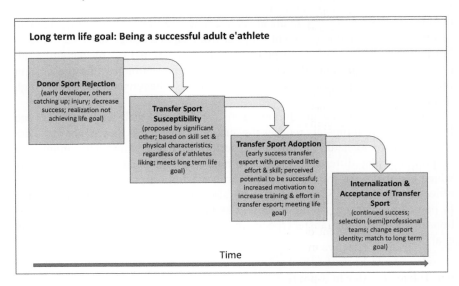

Figure 9.2 Adapted Adolescent Sport Talent model for e'athletes: Four transitions talented adolescent e'athletes travel from their primary to transfer esports.

9.6 Practical strategies and recommendations

It is always difficult giving recommendations for e'athletes or teams that are in the TID phase as there is no one-size-fits-all solution during this phase, as this is context-dependent. However, there are general rules of thumb that organisations can follow when identifying and recruiting new talent: (a) identify the needs of the team and (b) acknowledge that statistics paint a small fraction of the picture.

9.6.1 Identify the needs of the team

Organisations need to be purposeful in their search for new talent. To put the new roster in the best possible position, it is important to identify what is crucial for success in the roles within the team. Many coaches and managers will create a 'shopping list' to identify ideal characteristics needed from future players (Williams & Reilly, 2000). Furthermore, one must always be cognisant that athletes that perfectly match any criteria outlined are extremely rare; therefore, there is value in recruiting trialists that satisfy the criteria instead of holding out for an optimal solution (Klein & Calderwood, 1991).

9.6.2 Statistics paint a small fraction of the picture

Teams can fall into the trap of recruiting the 'best' performers available, based on a results-focussed methodology. Although there is value in accounting for one's statistical output, it's hard to accurately judge if this output was done in isolation or if those numbers could be inflated due to effort produced by teammates. Furthermore, statistics do not explain the social and psychological attributes of an individual. As many esports are team-based, it is important to find an athlete that supports the culture of the team and will provide meaningful engagement with their peers (coaches and teammates) (see Chapter 6). Across traditional sports and esports currently, there is a culture of developing 'super-teams' which is a practice of recruiting high-profiles players at their respective positions and it can lead to short-term success but has shown not to be a sustainable model for organisations. Furthermore, if those teams do not integrate properly with each other, the societal expectations placed on the team can further divide the team from within, causing performances to fall flat and goals to be left unmet. This in itself can pose a large difficulty for coaching staff because not only they are in a position where there may be too many fires to put out before progress can be made, but also it will place them in front of the talent market once again which is time-consuming and economically inefficient for organisations.

Suggestions for talent development are direly needed as research has already called for more effective methods. Many professional teams have main teams and academy teams, so there is a case to be made to combine the training of both those teams together. Like traditional sports where teams practise among themselves and create equal strength teams to practise technical and tactical principles, esports organisations can adopt a similar methodology to promote 'in-house' training and develop cohesive teams. Not only will this push the development of the academy team but will afford coaches to be more creative in their strategy by not having to worry about giving away information to potential opposition and can enable flexibility in practice duration.

References

Abbott, A., Button, C., Pepping, G. J., & Collins, D. (2005). Unnatural selection: Talent identification and development in sport. *Nonlinear Dynamics, Psychology, and Life Sciences, 9*(1), 61–88.

Abbott, A., & Collins, D. (2004). Eliminating the dichotomy between theory and practice in talent identification and development: Considering the role of psychology. *Journal of Sports Sciences, 22*(5), 395–408.

Abbott, C., Watson, M., & Birch, P. (2022). Perceptions of effective training practices in League of Legends: A qualitative exploration. *Journal of Electronic, 1*, 1–11.

Baker, J., Bagats, S., Büsch, D., Strauss, B., & Schorer, J. (2012). Training differences and selection in a talent identification system. *Talent Development & Excellence, 4*(1), 23–32.

Baker, J., Cobley, S., & Schorer, J. (2012). *Talent identification and development in sport: International perspectives*. Routledge.

Bloomfield, J., Polman, R., Butterly, R., & O'Donoghue, P. (2005). Analysis of age, stature, body mass, BMI and quality of elite soccer players from 4 European leagues. *Journal of Sports Medicine and Physical Fitness, 45*, 58–67.

Chase, W. G., & Simon, H. A. (1973). Perception in chess. *Cognitive Psychology, 4*(1), 55–81.

Collins, R., Collins, D., Macnamara, A., & Jones, M. (2014). Change of plan: An evaluation of the effectiveness and underlying mechanisms of successful talent transfer. *Journal of Sports Sciences, 32*, 1621–1630.

Conroy, E., Kowal, M., Toth, A. J., & Campbell, M. J. (2021). Boosting: Rank and skill deception in esports. *Entertainment Computing, 36*, 100393.

Craik, F. I. M., & Lockhart, R. S. (1972). Levels of processing: A framework for memory research. *Journal of Verbal Learning and Verbal Behavior, 11*, 671–684.

Den Hartigh, R. J., Hill, Y., & Van Geert, P. L. (2018). The development of talent in sports: A dynamic network approach. *Complexity* 2018, 9280154.

DiFrancisco-Donoghue, J., Balentine, J., Schmidt, G., & Zwibel, H. (2019). Managing the health of the eSport athlete: An integrated health management model. *BMJ Open Sport & Exercise Medicine, 5*(1), e000467.

Dimundo, F., Cole, M., Blagrove, R. C., Till, K., & Kelly, A. L. (2022). A multidisciplinary investigation into the talent development processes in an English Premiership rugby union academy: A preliminary study through an ecological lens. *Sports, 10*(2), 13.

Ericsson, K. A., Charness, N., Feltovich, R., & Hoffman, R. (2007). *The Cambridge handbook of expertise and expert performance*. Cambridge University Press.

Ericsson, K. A., Krampe, R. T., & Tesch-Römer, C. (1993). The role of deliberate practice in the acquisition of expert performance. *Psychological Review, 100*(3), 363–406.

Ericsson, K. A., & Lehmann, A. C. (1996). Expert and exceptional performance: Evidence of maximal adaptation to task constraints. *Annual Review of Psychology, 47*, 273–305.

Freeman, G., & Wohn, D. Y. (2019). Understanding eSports team formation and coordination. *Computer Supported Cooperative Work, 28*, 95–126.

Hayman, R., Polman, R., & Borkoles, E. (2021). Inter sport transfer: Experiences of high performing Australian adolescent athletes. *Journal of Expertise, 3*, 4.

Henriksen, K., & Stambulova, N. (2017). Creating optimal environments for talent development: A holistic ecological approach. In J. Baker, S. Cobley, J. Schorer, & N. Waitte (Eds.), *Routledge handbook of talent identification and development in sport* (pp. 270–284). Routledge.

Hyun, G. J., Shin, Y. W., Kim, B.-N, Cheong, J. H., Jin, S. N., & Han, D. H. (2013). Increased cortical thickness in professional on-line gamers. *Psychiatry Investigation, 10*, 388–392.

Klein, G. A., & Calderwood, R. (1991). Decision models: Some lessons from the field. *IEEE Transactions on Systems, Man, and Cybernetics, 21*(5), 1018–1026.

LeNorgant, E. J. (2019). *Sport-related anxiety and self-talk between traditional sports and esports* (Doctoral dissertation, California State University, Fresno).

MacNamara, A., & Collins, D. (2015). Second changes: Investigating athletes experiences of talent transfer. *PLoS One, 10*, 1–13.

Macnamara, B. N., Moreau, D., & Hambrick, D. Z. (2016). The relationship between deliberate practice and performance in sports: A meta-analysis. *Perspectives in Psychological Science, 11*, 333–350.

Meng-Lewis, Y., Wong, D., Zhao, Y., & Lewis, G. (2022). Understanding complexity and dynamics in the career development of eSports athletes. *Sport Management Review, 25*(1), 106–133.

Meylan, C., Cronin, J., Oliver, J., & Hughes, M. (2010). Talent identification in soccer: The role of maturity status on physical, physiological and technical characteristics. *International Journal of Sports Science & Coaching, 5*(4), 571–592.

Pluss, M. A., Novak, A. R., Bennett, K. J. M., McBride, I., Panchuk, D., Coutts, A. J., & Fransen, J. (2022). Examining the game-specific practice behaviors of professional and semi-professional esports players: A 52-week longitudinal study. *Computers in Human Behavior, 137*, 107421.

Roberts, A. H., Greenwood, D. A., Stanley, M., Humberstone, C., Iredale, F., & Raynor, A. (2019). Coach knowledge in talent identification: A systematic review and meta-synthesis. *Journal of Science and Medicine in Sport, 22*(10), 1163–1172.

Sabtan, B., Cao, S., & Paul, N. (2022). Current practices and challenges in coaching esports players: An interview study with League of Legends professional team coaches. *Entertainment Computing, 42*, 100481.

Salo, M. (2021). Career transitions of eSports athletes: A proposal for a research framework. In Information Resources Management Association (Ed.), *Research anthology on business strategies, health factors, and ethical implications in sports and eSports* (pp. 478–490). IGI Global.

Sanz-Matesanz, M., Gea-García, G. M., & Martínez-Aranda, L. M. (2023). Physical and psychological factors related to players health and performance in esports: A scoping review. *Computers in Human Behavior, 143*, 107698.

Sigmundsson, H., Trana, L., Polman, R., & Haga, M. (2017). What is trained develops! Theoretical perspective on skill learning. *Sports, 5*, 38.

Silva, M. C., Figueiredo, A. J., Simoes, F., Seabra, A., Natal, A., Vaeyens, R., Philippaerts, R., Cumming, S. P., & Malina, R. M. (2010). Discrimination of u-14 soccer players by level and position. *International Journal of Sports Medicine, 31*(11), 790–796.

Sorman, D. E., Dahl, K. E., Lindmark, D., Hansson, P., Vega-Mendoza, M., & Korning-Ljungberg, J. (2022). Relationship between Dota 2 expertise and decision-making ability. *PLoS One, 17*(3), e0264350.

Tanaka, S., Ikeda, H., Kasahara, K., Kato, R., Tsubomi, H., Sugawara, S. K., et al. (2013). Larger right posterior parietal volume in action video game experts: A behavioural and voxol-based morphometry (VBM) study. *PLoS One, 8*(6), e66998.

Thomas, C., Fellingham, G., & Vehrs, P. (2009). Development of a notational analysis system for selected soccer skills of a women's college team. *Measurement in Physical Education and Exercise Science, 13*(2), 108–121.

Williams, A. M., & Reilly, T. (2000). Talent identification and development in soccer. *Journal of Sports Sciences, 18*(9), 657–667.

10 Technology in esports

Matthew Watson and Craig McNulty

10.1 Introduction

By definition, esports is intertwined with technology, or more precisely digital, computer and information technology. This is clear in the earliest definition of esports, for example, from Wagner: "Esports is an area of sport activities in which people develop and train mental or physical abilities in the use of information and communication technologies" (2006, p. 3), as well as more recent descriptions, for example, from Scholz: "Esports is a cultural phenomenon with resemblance rooted in sports, media, entertainment, and culture, but emerged in a digitized environment" (Scholz, 2020). The evolution of video games into the competitive gaming industry of esports was accelerated by technological progress and developments like the personal computer, the internet, and the smartphone. In the early 90s, for example, relatively cheap technology allowed PCs to be connected in small networks and for players to play simultaneously–otherwise known as LAN parties. As improvements in the internet were made, there were exponential increases in players. For example, national investment in high-speed broadband internet in South Korea in the late 1990s drove the increasing usage of PC bangs (internet cafés) at a similar time as the release of the real-time strategy game StarCraft, which paved the way for the popularity of esports in the region and its competitive success today.

Technology is more than just the substrate of esports, it also brings opportunity. Esports is born digital and born global (Scholz, 2019), and for many businesses and organisations, this makes esports an extremely interesting proposition. Sports teams in particular have looked to take advantage of esports as a means to getting their brand online and connect with a younger audience, to varying degrees of success (Scholz et al., 2021). In education, esports is promoted as both a curriculum and an extracurricular programme in schools and universities, lauded for its potential to foster interest in–or even teach–science, technology, engineering, and math (STEM) subject and introduce gamers to "21st century skills and careers" (Rothwell & Shaffer, 2019, p. 3). It's worth noting that there is some criticism around the claims that involvement in esports per se improves digital competencies or interest in STEM subjects (in much the same way that playing a video game doesn't teach you to develop games), but esports does appear to hold promise as a vehicle to engage students in educational settings and improve social and emotional

DOI: 10.4324/9781003322382-10

competencies (Scott et al., 2021). In terms of the performance of players and teams, the push to achieve competitive success has driven advancements in various aspects of technology relating to esports, including developments in the hardware used, analytical and training tools, and arguably even social platforms such as Discord (a platform that is "at the center of the gaming universe"; Pierce, 2020).

10.2   Hardware

One of the most important technologies in esports is gaming hardware. Professional gamers require high-end computers (unless playing on mobile or console) with powerful processors and graphics cards in order to run their games smoothly without any lag or delays. They also need specialised peripherals such as gaming mice, keyboards, and headphones that provide them with precision and accuracy during gameplay. We'll consider these in more details now.

When purchasing or building a desktop computer or laptop for the purpose of esports participation, particularly where there are budgetary constraints, considerations should be made for the intended esports title(s) and their operational requirements from a hardware perspective. For example, the minimum and recommended hardware specifications for League of Legends is much less than that of Apex Legends (as of 2023). As well, as updated versions of games are released with improved graphics and higher processing requirements, it is beneficial to purchase or build a PC with predicted future needs in mind. The following section defines the key hardware components that will directly impact how efficiently a program operates (such as processors and cooling), as well as peripheral hardware that may impact performance (such as keyboards and monitors).

10.2.1   Computer parts

The primary computer parts are those which are necessary to run a program (such as an esports title), and include a central processing unit (CPU), a graphics processing unit (GPU), and a random access memory (RAM). These parts are all connected to a motherboard, with optimal operational temperatures maintained by a cooling system and powered by a dedicated power supply.

10.2.1.1   Central Processing Unit (CPU)

The CPU is responsible for executing program/software instructions. Currently, the two primary CPU manufacturers are Intel® and AMD®. Both of these manufacturers have a range of CPUs available depending on performance needs and budget. The Intel® Core™ processers range from the i3 series processor (~$100 USD), i5 series, i7 series, to the i9 series processor (~$700 USD), while the AMD® range in a similar fashion from the Ryzen™ 3 series (~$80 USD), 5 series, 7 series, to 9 series (~$480 USD). AMD® also manufactures an ultra-powerful Ryzen™ Threadripper™ series, with a price tag of ~$7,900 USD.

10.2.1.2 Graphics Processing Unit (GPU)

The GPU is similar to a CPU in its function, however, it functions in parallel (meaning multiple large processes can take place simultaneously) and its specialised design allows for the creation of images from large blocks of data. These images, or videos, are perceived by the user via a display monitor. The two leading manufacturers of GPUs (based on market share totalling nearly 100%) are AMD® and NVIDIA®. Similar to CPUs, GPUs have a range of models from both manufacturers to suit hardware performance needs and budget. The low-end GPUs are priced at ~$250 USD, with the top-end exceeding $2,500 USD. Higher-end GPUs (alongside other high-performance hardware) can produce higher frame rates without compromising graphics during gameplay. This is particularly beneficial to performance in esports titles where fast player reaction to on-screen stimuli is necessary.

10.2.1.3 Random Access Memory (RAM)

RAM is a form of working memory that, unlike other storage devices such as hard drives, can read and write information in short amount of time. This is where the operating system and current applications (such as a video game) are accessed while the computer is switched on. Total working memory volume is limited (compared to storage memory), and like other hardware, considerations for future proofing for updated game specifications should be considered. Modern computer RAM ranges from 4GB to 128GB with a price range of $25 USD to $500 USD.

10.2.2 Peripherals

Peripheral computer parts are those which don't drive the program but allow for user interaction and immersion. These include a display monitor(s), audio (speakers or microphones), and keyboard and mouse.

10.2.2.1 Display monitor

A display monitor, or screen, allows for the visual output of the GPU (and in part, CPU) processes. It is important to match the performance capacity of the GPU with the output capabilities of the monitor. That is, a high performing GPU is only as good as the monitor it is displaying on. The main considerations when purchasing a monitor for esports, in terms of potential impact to performance, are the resolution and pixel density, screen size, refresh rate, and panel type. **Resolution** of a modern standard wide screen monitor (16:9) is generally 1,920p × 1,080p (2K), 2,560p × 1,440p, or 3,840p × 2,160p (4K), with some small variations of these depending on manufacturer. With most esports titles, a high resolution is beneficial as it allows more discrete movement, clicking and aiming than a lower resolution monitor. **Pixel density** (pixels per square inch) is a product of resolution and screen size, where a higher pixel density will result in a smaller screen compared to a larger screen with the same resolution. **Screen size** is calculated as the diagonal measure along the face of the active screen. The optimal screen size for esports is dependent on a number of factors, such as esports title, distance the e'athlete's eyes will be from the screen, and whether the title will be played using a PC or console. Depending on preference/optimisation for performance, screen sizes generally range from 24 inch to 43 inch. **Refresh rate**, measured in Hertz (Hz), represents how many times per second a monitor can display a new image. To take advantage of a monitor with a high refresh rate, a high-performing GPU is necessary to maintain high frame rates. The recommended minimum monitor refresh rate for esports is 144 Hz, with newer high-end monitors with 360 Hz refresh rates now becoming quite common. Lastly, **panel type** is the technology used in the monitor's liquid crystal display to produce an image. The three panel types are twisted nematic (TN), in-plane switching (IPS), and vertical alignment (VA). TN is the oldest technology, with the best response time, but with a more acute viewing angle. IPS generally produces the best colours and wider viewing angles, but with a slower response time. VA is known for having the best contrast ratio, with strong colour, making them ideal for high dynamic range content. For esports performance, fast response time will be of more importance than colour and viewing angle in most cases. Therefore, a TN panel would be a good choice when purchasing a display monitor, however, the response time of VA panel is only slightly slower than that of a TN. For immersive, colour-rich (and generally non-competitive) video gameplay, an IPS panel would be a practical solution.

10.2.2.2 Audio

While both headsets and external speakers can create a more immersive gaming environment than most in-built laptop and desktop speakers, a headset with microphone is the essential option for many esports titles due to the necessity of in-game communication between players of the same team. There is a vast range of options available for headphones with built-in microphones. For use in esports, some key considerations are:

1   Sound quality and acuity – depending on the esports title, simply being able to clearly hear teammates and respond, while listening to general game audio is enough, such as in League of Legends or Defence of the Ancients 2. However, some titles such as Call of Duty and Counter Strike: Global Offence are reliant on much higher acuity of sound, and surround sound, to allow the player to hear directional noises such as enemy footsteps, reloading, and item-use nearby.
2   Sound isolation – the quality of the build of the headset will determine sound isolation, that is, the headband and earphones should remain secure on the head, even while moving. It is also important that a strong seal is created between the earphones and the player's head to avoid excessive environmental noise entering the ear.
3   Microphone – either an attached boom microphone, or detachable 3.5 mm jack or USB microphone is necessary for most esports communication. It is suggested that players sound check and adjust operating system sound output volumes to be sure that others can clearly hear what is being said.

10.2.2.3 Keyboard

Often the best esports keyboard is the one which the player finds the most comfortable. However, there are some key considerations when purchasing a keyboard for gaming. Firstly, a wired keyboard (as opposed to Bluetooth®) is necessary to avoid keystroke lag which can slow the response time of key presses to what happens in game, as well as potentially missing keystrokes. A mechanical keyboard, rather than a non-mechanical (or membrane) keyboard, is necessary due to its improved response times. Mechanical keyboards may use linear, tactile, or clicky keys, and may be full-sized, tenkeyless (full-size without a number pad), or compact. Keyboard size and mechanical key-type choice are mostly determined by what the player finds comfortable.

10.2.2.4 Mouse

For most esports titles, an ideal mouse will be a wired, lightweight six-button configuration with accurate sensor tracking and no mouse sensitivity buttons. As with a keyboard, a wired mouse is the ideal option to avoid unnecessary lag. As many elite esports athletes opt for low mouse sensitivity (or low dpi [dots per inch]) and a large mouse movement area, it's important to opt for a light-weight mouse to help mitigate muscular fatigue and repetitive strain. A 6-button configuration of the left and right click buttons, middle mouse scroll wheel and button, and two side buttons is the common configuration for most esports titles. As the majority of esports games and competitions do not allow for assigning multiple actions to a single mouse button (macroing), the use of multiple-button gaming mouses (sometimes upward of 20 or more individual buttons) is superfluous and adds unwanted mass to the mouse. Accurate sensor tracking is essential for discrete cursor, aiming, or avatar movement, while additional sensitivity control buttons are avoided so as to not mis-click during play.

10.3 Software, websites and AI

Hardware and software components are both fundamental elements in esports that have to be integrated. There are various layers of software in most modern consumer electronic devices, from the device's operating system ("closest" to the hardware) to the end-user applications (the games themselves). While a full explanation of the various layers of software and their integration is beyond the scope of this chapter, it may be useful for the reader to be aware of some key software and platforms used within esports (Table 10.1).

Esports also relies heavily on data analytics technology. Teams use data analytics tools to analyse their opponents' strategies and gameplay patterns to gain a competitive advantage over them. This technology helps teams identify weaknesses in their opponents' playstyle and develop counter-strategies accordingly. Artificial intelligence (AI) in particular is showing promise as a means to analyse data and provide feedback to guide strategic decision-making, often in real time. Consider the following from the founder of iTero Gaming start-up Jack Williams (Box 10.1):

Table 10.1 Key Software and Platforms Used in League of Legends

League of Legends (MOBA)	
Software/Website	Description
Blitz/Mobalytic/U.GG	In Game Companion
	• Provides insights into player performance/habits
	• Collates game data of teammates/opposition
	• Provides in-game overlays (e.g., CS per min, Jungle timers)
OP.GG	Player Search Engine
	• Can look at other players' match history, win rate, and champion pick rate
	• Effective tool for player scouting
	• Also has overall patch data (champion pick rate, win rates, build paths)
Oracle's Elixir	Professional Esports Data Base
	• Collates game data from professional leagues
	• In-depth player, team, and champion analytics
Mobafire/Probuilds	Champion Guide/Build Forum
	• Player-created guides/information regarding champion playstyle, matchups, itemisation, and runes
iTtero. GG	Drafting AI Tool
	• Provides best possible draft solutions for players live during champ selection

Valorant (FPS)	
Software/Website	Description
Tracker. GG	In-Game Companion & Player Search Engine
	• Provides live data about teammates, opposition, and performance insights
Vlr. GG	Professional Valorant Database
	In-depth and comprehensive player, team, and agent statistics
Tip Genius	In-Game Coach
	• Provides live tips for players to help improve performance and gameplay

Miscellaneous	
Software/Website	Description
Insights Capture	Gameplay Recording Software
	• Easily record and store gameplay from player's POV to easily analyse gameplayer afterwards
Steam	Digital Distribution Platform/Gaming Software Ecosystem
	• While not strictly speaking an example of gaming software, Steam has an important role in any discussion of technology in video games and esports as a common storefront for distributing games. The Steam Workshop also allows users to make modifications ("mods"), maps and items for a variety of games and share them

---

Box 10.1   From Jack Williams from iTero Gaming on AI in esports

The rise of Artificial Intelligence feels like an inevitability in all walks of life, yet to me there are few industries in a better position to exploit this technology than esports. The ease, accessibility, and sheer amount of data is profound. Thousands of data points from millions of games are being captured every single day. This includes the games played by the very players who step on stage each weekend to play professionally.

In traditional sports, AI has already found its footing, from player scouting to match analysis, and major teams are investing heavily in this new competitive advantage. Yet, esports finds itself in an even better position as it already lives inside the virtual world, removing the need to translate complex physical rules into code before the work can start.

So, what will AI look like in esports? First, it can do what it does best; pattern recognition. Whether that is identifying the early signs of a future all-star player long before the eyes of the world fall on them, finding an exploitable weakness in an upcoming opponent's game plan or helping optimise pre-game strategising and decision-making. What previously would take a coach or analyst hours upon hours of sifting through game footage and statistics can be compressed into a few seconds of computerised review, identifying key trends that are too complex for the human eye.

However, that is only the beginning. Eventually, AI will be able to master any game it touches. It will become the ultimate training partner, capable of playing beyond any level seen before. It could even be taught to replicate a specific team, imitating their playstyles and allowing others to "scrim" against it again and again.

With all that being said, I still believe esports will always need coaches. AI will act as the bionic arm, enhancing the user – but never replacing them.

10.4 Ping

Ping (sometimes called latency or lag) is a term used to describe the delay between a user's input through their device (i.e., computer or controller) and the response from the server. Ping is a factor that can greatly enhance or debilitate one's gaming experience. It is measured in milliseconds (ms) and the lower the number, the smoother the human-computer interaction. In most professional contexts, major competitions are hosted offline and teams will compete in a studio or on a local area network (LAN) server. This enables players to compete on low latency (less than 20 ms is considered ideal for gaming), allowing for fairer competition as the time it takes from a keystroke or button press and action on screen is reduced and equal across everyone (Ross & Fisackerly, 2023).

However, when teams are not in the studio, or for the casual gamer, ping can be an uncontrollable variable. There are a few factors that determine a player's ping, those being; (a) a player's internet speeds (i.e., upload and download), (b) physical distance to server, (c) local internet traffic (bandwidth), and (d) type of connection to the internet (i.e., Wi-Fi or Ethernet). Many esports divide the globe into various regions to afford equal opportunity for players to experience games on low latency. However, this can also be a limiting factor, as the infrastructure for regions may not be equal, and in certain esports titles can limit the opportunity for players to connect and play with friends across the world. In FPS and racing games especially, a lower ping (at least less than 50 ms) is considered crucial to stay competitive with other players.

10.4.1 Example 1 – League of Legends (NA)

Yilliang "Doublelift" Peng, a veteran player within the North American League of Legends scene, is one of the many pro players who is vocal about the issue regarding the ping, and its impacts on practice. Most, if not all professional teams within the LCS are located in California, whereas the servers for LoL are based in Chicago. This poses a hindrance for players as they frequently swap between a low ping environment (tournament realm; 5–10 ms) and a high ping environment (solo queue; 60 + ms) which can affect the playstyle and quality of performance.

10.4.2 Example 2 – Call of duty Warzone VPN incident

Call of Duty: Warzone, a free-to-play battle royale game was all the hype for gamers. It also brought a highly competitive esports spectrum allowing streamers, professional and rising stars to compete against each other for cash prizes. However, during this time, there was a cloud of controversy that loomed over the competitive integrity of its participants. As the game used skill-based matchmaking (SBMM) to create evenly skilled lobbies, there were allegations that players might be using virtual private networks (VPN) to mask their location and bypass the accuracy of SBMM. This in theory would place competitors in 'easier' lobbies, where their chances of winning and obtaining a high kill score, both of which are crucial factors in determining success, was greater.

10.5 Potential downsides

Of course, surrounding the use of digital and computer technology within esports is a general discussion about the impacts on health and well-being, particularly amongst younger people. Public health messages and research papers highlight the potential benefits of engaging with digital technology in terms of developing digital competencies and engaging with STEM subjects, but also raise concerns about the potential impacts of screen time, internet and social media usage on social, emotional, cognitive health and development (Straker et al., 2018). The advantage that esports has in this regard is its social nature, in that it involves interaction with at least another person, thus individuals can develop interpersonal and intrapersonal competencies through participation in esports (Trotter et al., 2022). Furthermore, recognising that successful and sustainable esports performance requires players to be in good physical and mental health, there is also a push for greater involvement of trained practitioners in these areas (e.g., Sport & Exercise Psychologists; Leis et al., 2023; Watson et al., 2021).

One potential downside that might get overlooked in esports, particularly as teams seek to innovate and integrate new technology into their performance approach, is the potential risk of dehumanising e'athletes through an overreliance on data and information technology. This is a concern that has previously been raised in sport in light of the myriad ways in which performance can be monitored, tracked, and analysed (Cronin et al., 2019; Woods et al., 2021). With the vast amount of game data available and popularity of physiological monitoring technologies in esports at present, the potential to reduce individual performance down into isolated statistics or dashboards is arguably higher than in sport. However, doing so risks disengaging the players from less quantifiable features of the performance environment, detracting from potential learning and developmental experiences (Woods et al., 2021) and further heightening players' awareness of metrics such as their rank (Abbott et al., 2022). Coaches and other support staff in esports may have an important role here in emphasising that technological devices and apps represent a useful resource to aid understanding of performance, but do not represent all facets of performance nor the (complex) interplay between them.

10.6 Conclusion

In conclusion, technology plays a fundamental and facilitative role in esports by enabling players to compete at the highest level while providing fans with an immersive viewing experience. From high-end gaming hardware to streaming platforms, data analytics tools, and virtual reality technology – all these technologies have contributed significantly to the growth of this industry over the years. As technology continues to evolve rapidly, we can expect even more exciting developments that will shape the future of esports.

References

Abbott, C., Watson, M., & Birch, P. (2022). Perceptions of effective training practices in league of legends: A qualitative exploration. *Journal of Electronic Gaming and Esports, 1*(1), 1–11.

Cronin, C., Whitehead, A. E., Webster, S., & Huntley, T. (2019). Transforming, storing and consuming athletic experiences: A coach's narrative of using a video application. *Sport, Education and Society, 24*(3), 311–323. https://doi.org/10.1080/13573322.2017.1355784

Leis, O., Watson, M., Swettenham, L., Pedraza-Ramirez, I., & Lautenbach, F. (2023). Stress Management strategies in esports: An exploratory online survey on applied practice. *Journal of Electronic Gaming and Esports, 1*(1), 1–11.

Pierce, D. (2020, December 31). How discord (somewhat accidentally) invented the future of the internet. *Protocol.* https://www.protocol.com/discord

Ross, W. J., & Fisackerly, W. (2023). Do we need esports ecology? comparisons of environmental impacts between traditional sport and esports. *Journal of Electronic Gaming and Esports*, *1*(1), 1–7.

Rothwell, G., & Shaffer, M. (2019). eSports in K-12 and Post-Secondary schools. *Education Sciences, 9*(2), 105.

Scholz, T. M. (2019). *Esports is business. Management in the world of competitive gaming.* Cham, Switzerland: Palgrave Macmillan.

Scholz, T. M. (2020). Deciphering the World of eSports. *JMM International Journal on Media Management, 22*(1), 1–12. https://doi.org/10.1080/14241277.2020.1757808

Scott, M. J., Summerley, R., Besombes, N., Connolly, C., Gawrysiak, J., Halevi, T., ... & Williams, J. P. (2021). Foundations for esports curricula in higher education. In *Proceedings of the 2021 Working Group Reports on Innovation and Technology in Computer Science Education*, New York (pp. 27–55).

Straker, L., Zabatiero, J., Danby, S., Thorpe, K., & Edwards, S. (2018). Conflicting guidelines on young children's screen time and use of digital technology create policy and practice dilemmas. *The Journal of Pediatrics, 202*, 300–303.

Trotter, M. G., Coulter, T. J., Davis, P. A., Poulus, D. R., & Polman, R. (2022). Examining the impact of school esports program participation on student health and psychological development. *Frontiers in Psychology*, *12*, 6608.

Wagner, M. G. (2006). On the scientific relevance of eSports. In *Proceedings of the 2006 International Conference on Internet Computing and Conference on Computer Game Development, International Conference on Internet Computing*, Las Vegas, NV (pp. 437–440).

Watson, M., Abbott, C., & Pedraza-Ramirez, I. (2021). A parallel approach to performance and sport psychology work in esports teams. *International Journal of Esports, 2*(2), 1–6.

Woods, C. T., Araújo, D., Davids, K., & Rudd, J. (2021). From a technology that replaces human perception–Action to one that expands it: some critiques of current technology use in sport. *Sports Medicine - Open, 7*(1). https://doi.org/10.1186/s40798-021-00366-y

11 Social environment and health in esports

Remco Polman and Kabir Bubna

11.1 Introduction

Considering the growth of esports in terms of participants, spectators, and revenue, it is important to consider its role in the wider society. Although the main cohort interested in esports are school children, adolescents, and young adults (Yin et al., 2020), its influence is permeating many aspects of society. This includes its presence in universities, schools, media, businesses, and even technological developments (e.g., Reitman et al., 2020).

Participation in esports, much like traditional sports, provides an opportunity for participants to reap a myriad of social benefits. Although seen predominantly as entertainment and a hobby for those involved, esports has the potential to provide a sense of community to those passionate about gaming. Within these communities, there are plentiful opportunities for social interaction with fellow gamers, and it is not uncommon to see players form close bonds with each other leading to long-lasting friendships (Hamari & Sjöblom, 2017).

For the casual e'athlete, interaction within esports also has the potential to develop a multitude of transferable skills (Trotter et al., 2022). Competitive esports titles such as League of Legends (LoL), Overwatch, and Counter-Strike: Global Offensive (CS:GO) are examples of team-based esports. It has the potential to teach individuals the importance of teamwork, effective communication, conflict resolution, and challenging their problem-solving capabilities (Leung & Chu, 2023). These skills are highly transferable to many professional (i.e., school or work) and personal situations.

With esports being virtual, it opens the doors for global participation. It is not uncommon for e'athletes to connect and play with members from vastly different cultures and localities, allowing individuals to embrace diversity and inclusivity. This also plays a significant role in the integration of esports into wider society. Furthermore, esports provides a platform for e'athletes to be recognised for their skills, with less focus on their nationality, upbringing, values, and beliefs. This aspect can help garner attention to the barriers currently placed in society for marginalised groups (i.e., women, LGBTQ+, POC, and disabled).

DOI: 10.4324/9781003322382-11

11.2 Esports and health

An area in which esports differs from traditional sport is its physical and psychological health risks and benefits. Although there are numerous health risks in sport including musculoskeletal injuries and concussion, there is the view that esports is associated with chronic conditions like obesity (except exergames) and other negative metabolic consequences (VandeWater et al., 2004). In addition, concerns have been raised regarding sedentary behaviour, psychological development, and physical health and wellbeing (Shum et al., 2021). Although there is a cause and effect between increased screen time and obesity in children and adolescents (e.g., Robinson et al., 2017), recent meta-analysis found conflicting results for gaming. One meta-analysis showed that gaming was not associated with an increased Body Mass Index (BMI) or reduced physical activity behaviour (Marker et al., 2022) whereas another meta-analysis showed an association between gaming and increased BMI (Chan et al., 2022). Although both meta-analysis were based on mainly gaming studies, more recently Trotter et al. (2022) showed in a sample of 188 secondary school adolescents no differences in physical activity or sport behaviour or their self-perceived health between those who played esports and matched controls. In addition, in large sample (n = 1,772) of e'athletes, it was found that they were more likely to be classified in the normal weight category (based on their BMI) compared to normative data. Although a large proportion (80%) did not meet the World Health Organization (WHO) physical activity guidelines (> 2.5 hours per week of moderate or vigorous physical activity), the sample reported much lower smoking and alcohol drinking frequencies compared to normative data (Trotter et al., 2020). Finally, in a study by Rudolf et al. (2020) on mainly young, well-educated, male gamers and e'athletes, it was found that most played sport, 66.9% met the WHO physical activity guidelines and had a similar BMI distribution compared to the German population.

Current, mainly self-report, findings suggest that esports is not associated with increased levels of obesity or reduced sport and physical activity participation. However, more objective studies are required which use accelerometers or pedometers to measure physical activity behaviour and objective measures to assess body composition.

There is some emerging evidence that e'athletes have disturbed sleeping patterns. For example, e'athletes have reported lower average sleeping times, delayed sleep timing, reduced sleep quality (e.g., waking up during sleep episodes), and daytime sleepiness (Gomes et al., 2021; Lee et al., 2020; Rudolf et al., 2020). Similar findings (reduced sleep duration and quality, delayed sleep timing and higher levels of daytime sleepiness) have also been found in video gamers (Kemp et al., 2021). However, reduced sleeping time is common in those transitioning from adolescence to adulthood (Kuula et al., 2019). As such it is unclear whether the findings are due to playing esports or because of the general age range of the participants in these studies.

Because of the international nature of esports allowing e'athletes to play across time-zones (e.g., during the night) in conjunction with the excessive training hours reported in the literature, this can result in maladaptive sleeping behaviours. Poor sleeping behaviours have been associated with reduced cognitive functioning (e.g., reduced reaction time and slower processing of information) (Lowe et al., 2017), reduced academic and athletic performance (e.g., Walsh et al., 2021), and poorer mental health outcomes (Scott et al., 2021). As such it would be important for e'athletes and their coaches to adopt adaptive sleeping behaviours.

Research also suggests that excessive gaming is associated with increased consumption of sugary drinks and savory snacks (e.g., Chaput et al., 2011). In addition, e'athletes have reported low fruit and vegetable consumption although did not differ from the German population (Rudolf et al., 2020). A healthy diet in combination with regular physical activity and sleep are predictors of physical health, cognition (note, obesity is negatively related to cognition) and performance in adolescents (e.g., Naveed et al., 2020). In particular the consumption of fruit and vegetables might help e'athletes to enhance their cognition and esports performance.

Considering the growth in e'athletes and spectators in esports, it would make this an ideal platform for influencing health behaviours, in particular, in groups which are hard to reach (Polman et al., 2018). To this end, those who develop esports have made use of psychological theories and concepts to ensure the e-athletes keep on playing. For example, many esports make use of continuous (for new behaviours) and intermitted (already established behaviours) reinforcement schedules which are extremely effective in stimulating the reward pathway in our brain. However, through working with game developers, esports clubs and organisations, and influencers it might be possible to, for example, to promote healthy eating programs or physical activity programs to groups who previously have been hard to influence. In addition, the importance of physical and psychosocial health is crucial for performance and injury prevention. As such, elite e'athletes could act as role-models to bring about health behaviour change in grassroots e'athletes. As such esports has the potential to promote and change population health (see Polman et al., 2018).

11.3 Professional level

For those that interact in a more competitive and organised form of esports, players will work in similar environments to sporting teams. E'athletes will develop collaboration skills and develop an understanding how to work within authoritative structures (i.e., coaches and managers). Professional esports teams are often managed in a similar way to professional sport teams. They include coaches, psychologists, nutritionist, physical trainers and data-analysts to help to optimise the performance of the e'athletes. As mentioned previously in this book, current training practices appear to be less than optimal which has resulted in significant health concerns in elite e'athletes. Based on their research, Madden and Harteveld (2021) proposed a Health in Esports model. This is based on four factors: (1) physical health (injury, pain, and breaks), (2) psychological wellness (stress (family/friends/self-inflicted), anxiety, and burnout), (3) support (family, teammates, friends, and self-perceived), and (4) daily routine (practice and sleep). The e'athletes in this study were particularly concerned about their physical health (obesity) due to a lack of exercise and nutrition planning. Interestingly, those who were engaged in regular exercise reported fewer injuries. Together with the increasing practice time at the elite level, Madden and Harteveld (2021) recommend to train smarter and not harder by including break times for e'athletes to recover and include exercises in their training programs to prevent overuse injuries and enhance physical and mental wellbeing. Similar suggestions have been made by DiFrancisco-Donoghue et al. (2019). They also advocate exercise as a means to avoid overuse injuries and the incorporation of health professionals to diagnose and treat e'athletes in their return to play.

Health monitoring either by the individual e'athlete or team health professionals would be an important strategy to enhance performance and wellbeing of elite e-athletes. This would include both the physical and psychological health and welfare (see Chapter 4 on stress and coping). An important issue is the concept of gaming disorder, a pattern of gaming behaviour (digital or video) characterised by impaired control over gaming, increasing priority given to gaming over other activities to the extent that gaming takes precedence over other interests and daily activities, and continuation or escalation of gaming despite the occurrence of negative consequences (WHO, 2018: 11th Revision of the International Classification of Diseases (ICD-11)). Similar to exercise addiction, it is questionable whether those at the elite level can be classified as suffering from gaming disorder. As a comparison, marathon runners will also engage in significant time training and practising. It is estimated they engage in up to 220 km per week just running across 11–14 training sessions (Haugen et al., 2022). However, it is argued that this is required to achieve marathon running at the elite level. Most elite e'athletes will also argue that the training volume they engage in is required to achieve and stay at the elite level. As such the concept of gaming addiction might me a misnomer for elite e'athletes.

11.4 Grassroots level

There is an increasing level of organisation of esports at the grassroots level. Although most e'athletes still compete through private online communities, there are now other opportunities for e'athletes to train and compete in different organisational settings and structures. This is, for example, through new esports associations, existing sport organisations, schools and universities both online and in physical locations. In some countries, esports have been part of the school curriculum (Ortiz de Gortari, 2019). There is currently little research on what e'athletes want or on comparisons to the benefits of online versus in-person participation in esports. However, based on sport research it is known that being a member of sport clubs or community sport participation has psychological and social benefits above and beyond being just physically active (Eime et al., 2013). It is easier to be connected to others in the physical world and connectedness proves to be one of the strongest protective factors for physical, mental, and social health and wellbeing (House et al., 1988). For example, higher levels of connectedness are associated with higher self-esteem, empathy, and better emotional regulation whereas low social connections are associated with higher susceptibility to anxiety and depression and increased antisocial behaviour and violence. Physical organisations also make it easier to provide coaching and information on aspects like diet, sleep, exercise, and psychological skills.

The introduction of esports in schools and universities makes it possible to develop and assess the introduction of healthy and safe engagement in esports. For example, e'athletes can be asked to engage in courses to reduce online toxicity or exercise regimes to reduce overuse injuries. To this end, Trotter et al. (2022) conducted a study which examined the impact of a school esports programme on the student's health and psychological development. Although the study was negatively impacted by the COVID-19 lockdowns, it showed that at baseline there were no differences between those students who participated in esports and the matched controls except for sport participation. Additionally, post-test decreases in the connection factor and physical activity behaviour were lower in both groups mainly due to the COVID-19 lockdowns. It will be important for future research to examine whether esports, like sport, can also result in the development of self-regulation skills and positive youth development and which setting (e.g., school, club, and online) is most conducive for such developments.

Ultimately local grassroots models need to be developed either online or face-to-face which caters to e'athletes at all levels and considers performance, physical and mental health, and wellbeing of the e'athletes.

References

Chan, G., Huo, Y., Kelly, S., Leung, J., Tisdale, C., & Gullo, M. (2022). The impact of esports and online video gaming on lifestyle behaviours in youth: A systematic review. *Computer in Human Behavior, 15*, 106974.

Chaput, J. P., Visby, T., Nyby, S., Klingenberg, L., Gregersen, N. T., Tremblay, A., Astrup, A., & Sjödin, A. (2011). Video game playing increases food intake in adolescents: a randomized crossover study. *The American Journal of Clinical Nutrition, 93*(6), 1196–1203. https://doi.org/10.3945/ajcn.110.008680

DiFrancisco-Donoghue, J., Balentine, J., Schmidt, G., & Zwibel, H. (2019). Managing the health of the esport athlete: An integrated health and management model. *BMJ Open: Sport & Exercise Medicine, 5*, e000467.

Eime, R. M., Young, J. A., Harvey, J. T., Charity, M. J., & Payne, W. R. (2013). A systematic review of the psychological and social benefits of participation in sport for children and adolescents: Informing development of a conceptual model of health through sport. *International Journal of Behavioral Nutrition and Physical Activity, 10*, 98.

Gomes, M., Narciso, F., de Mello, M., & Esteves, A. (2021). Identifying electronic-sport athletes' sleep-wake cycle characteristics. *Chronobiology International, 38*(7), 1002–1009.

Hamari, J., & Sjöblom, M. (2017). What is esports and why do people watch it? *Internet Research, 27*(2), 211–232.

Haugen, T., Sandbakk, O., Seiler, S., & Tonnessen, E. (2022). The training characteristics of world-class distance runners: An integration of scientific literature and results-proven practice. *Sports Medicine Open, 8*, 46.

House, J. S., Landis, K. R., & Umberson, D. (1988). Social relationships and health. *Science, 241*, 540–545.

Kemp, C., Pienaar, P., Rosslee, D., Lipinska, G., Roden, L., & Rae, D. (2021). Sleep in habitual adult video gamers: A systematic review. *Frontiers in Neuroscience, 15,* 781351.

Kuula, L., Gradisar, M., Martinmäki, K., Richardson, C., Bonnar, D., Bartel, K., Lang, C., Leinonen, L., & Pesonen, A. (2019). Using big data to explore worldwide trends in objective sleep in the transition to adulthood. *Sleep Medicine, 62,* 69–76.

Lee, S., Bonnar, D., Roane, B., Gradisar, M., Jang, E., & Suh, S. (2020). Sleep characteristics and mood of professional esports athletes: A multi-national study. *Sleep, 43,* A75–A76.

Leung, K.-M., & Chu, W. (2023). eSports participation among Hong Kong middle-aged and older adults: A qualitative study. *Human Behavior and Emerging Technologies, 2023,* 6798748.

Lowe, C., Safati, A., & Hall, P. (2017). The neurocognitive consequences of sleep restriction: A meta-analytic review. *Neuroscience and Biobehavioral Reviews, 80,* 586–604.

Madden, D., and Harteveld, C. 2021. "Constant Pressure of Having to Perform": Exploring player health concerns in Esports. In *Proceedings of the 2021 CHI Conference on Human Factors in Computing Systems (CHI '21)* (Article 324, pp. 1–14). New York, NY: Association for Computing Machinery. https://doi.org/10.1145/3411764.3445733

Marker, C., Gnambs, T., & Appel, M. (2022). Exploring the myth of the chubby gamer: A meta-analysis on sedentary video gaming and body mass. *Social Science & Medicine, 301,* 112325.

Naveed, S., Lakka, T., & Haapla, E. A. (2020). An overview on the association between health behaviors and brain health in children and adolescents with special reference to diet quality. *International Journal of Environmental Research and Public Health, 17,* 953.

Ortiz de Gortari, A. B. (2019). *Esports in Nordic schools: Survey results – wave 1.* SLATE Research Report 2019-4. Bergen, Norway: Centre for the Science of Learning & Technology.

Polman, R. C. J., Trotter, M., Poulus, D., & Borkoles, E. (2018). eSport: Friend or Foe? In S. Gobel et al. (Eds.), *Joint Conference on Serious Games 2018 LNCS* (Chapter 1, pp. 1–6). Switzerland: Springer Nature.

Reitman, J. G., Anderson-Coto, M. J., Wu, M., Lee J. S., & Steinkuehler, C. (2020). Esports research: A literature review. *Games and Culture, 15*(1), 32–50.

Robinson, T. N., Banda, J. A., Hale, L., Lu, A. S., Fleming-Milici, F., Calvert, S. L., & Wartella, E. (2017). Screen media exposure and obesity in children and adolescents. *Pediatrics, 140*(Suppl 2), S97–S101.

Rudolf, K., Bickmann, P., Fröböse, I., Tholl, C., Wechsler, K., & Grieben, C. (2020). Demographics and health behavior of video game and eSports players in Germany: The eSports study 2019. *International Journal of Environmental Research and Public Health, 17*(6), 1870. https://doi.org/10.3390/ijerph17061870

Scott, J., Kallestad, H., Vedaa, O., Sivertsen, B., & Etain, B. (2021). Sleep disturbances and first onset of major mental disorders in adolescence and early adulthood: A systematic review and meta-analysis. *Sleep Medicine Reviews, 57,* 101429.

Shum, H.-L., Lee, C.-H., & Cheun, J. C.-S. (2021). Should esports be a co-curricular activity in school? *Child Schools, 43,* 61–63.

Trotter, M. G., Coulter, T. J., Davis, P. A., Poulus, D. R., & Polman, R. (2020). The association between esports participation, health and physical activity behaviour. *International Journal of Environmental Research and Public Health, 17,* 7329.

Trotter, M. G., Coulter, T. J., Davis, P. A., Poulus, D. R., & Polman, R. (2022). Examining the impact of school esports program participation on student health and psychological development. *Frontiers in Psychology, 12,* 807341.

Vandewater, E. A., Shim, M.-S., & Caplovitz, A. G. (2004). Linking obesity and activity level with children's television and video game use. *Journal of Adolescence, 27*(1), 71–85.

Walsh, N. P., Halson, S. L., Sargent, C., Roach, G. D., Nedelec, M., Gupta, L., et al. (2021). Sleep and the athlete: Narrative review and 2021 expert consensus recommendations. *British Journal of Sports Medicine, 55*, 356–368.

World Health Organisation, 2018. Gaming disorder. Available from https://www.who.int/standards/classifications/frequently-asked-questions/gaming-disorder

Yin, K., Zi, Y., Zhuang, W., Gao, Y., Tong, Y., Song, L., & Liu, Y. (2020). Linking esports to health risks and benefits: Current knowledge and future research needs. *Journal of Sport and Health Science, 9*, 485–488.

12 Safeguarding, cheating, and gambling

Matthew Watson and Craig McNulty

12.1 Safeguarding in esports

The safety and protection of young people and vulnerable adults is a crucial concern in all areas of life, and this is no different in gaming and esports. However, as an industry, there is a pressing need to increase our focus on the safety and protection of these groups in gaming and esports, for numerous reasons. First, and obviously, online gaming and esports continue to attract huge numbers of new players, viewers and fans, many of whom are from a younger demographic. Second, esports is a relatively new industry that has emerged largely on its own without any oversight from governing organisations that typically enforce safeguarding principles in other areas of youth activity (e.g., sport; Rhind et al., 2015). In other words, esports is playing catch-up to other areas of youth activity in which safeguarding conventions and standards are commonplace. Third, esports was 'born digital' (Scholz, 2019), and therefore, shares many of the same risks associated with internet usage and being online, such as bullying, receiving unsolicited messages of a sexual nature, and exposure to potentially harmful user-generated content (Livingstone et al., 2011). Such risks are perhaps heightened by the various additional channels (e.g., digital social/messaging platforms) through which young people and vulnerable adults can be privately contacted under the guise of esports-related activity.

Importantly, the purpose of this chapter is not to deter individuals or organisations from entering esports or working with young people. Far from it, the "involvement of more children and young people in esports is something to be celebrated and encouraged" (Hatter, 2020), as esports has the potential to promote a host of opportunities and positive outcomes for young people. The purpose of this chapter is, instead, to foster further awareness of, and attention on, safeguarding in esports with a view to making esports a safer and more sustainable environment in which young people and vulnerable adults can thrive. Indeed, this is the promise of esports (Box 12.1).

12.1.1 What is safeguarding?

Safeguarding refers to the measures taken to protect vulnerable individuals from harm, abuse, or neglect. Typically, the primary focus of safeguarding is on children and vulnerable adults who may be at particular risk due to their age, physical or

DOI: 10.4324/9781003322382-12

Box 12.1 Important definitions

CHILDREN are defined as persons under the age of 18 years old. They are protected under the United Nations Convention on the Rights of the Child, which has been adopted by 197 nations.

A VULNERABLE ADULT is any person aged 18 years old or over who may be unable to protect him- or herself against harassment, abuse, neglect or exploitation as a result of their age, disability, gender, or other factor.

---

mental health, disability, or other factors. Safeguarding broadly involves identifying potential risks, taking steps to prevent them from occurring and the process of managing cases when they occur. Of the many forms of safeguarding, practices can range from designing policies and procedures to prevent abuse or neglect, training programmes for staff working with vulnerable individuals, risk assessments, and support services for victims of abuse or neglect.

In recent years, there has been increasing research attention on safeguarding in sport, particularly concerning abusive relationships (Rhind et al., 2015). While being viewed as a very positive experience, many young people report negative experiences through their sport participation. For example, in a study of 6,000 young people in the United Kingdom, Alexander et al. (2011) reported that 75% had experienced emotional abuse, 29% sexual harassment, 24% physical abuse, 10% self-harm, and 3% sexual abuse (see also Box 12.2 for a list of definitions of the different forms of abuse and neglect). In their review of safeguarding cases in sport in the United Kingdom, Rhind et al. (2015) identified that 652 cases were managed by the lead welfare officers of sport national governing bodies in 2011. Of these cases, 91% of alleged perpetrators were male, 65% of victims were male, and 89% of victims were under 18 years old. These findings are particularly alarming for esports when considering that it is often described as a predominantly young, male demographic.

At present, there are a few prominent areas for concern in regard to safeguarding in esports. For example, the esports industry is unregulated and ungoverned. Indeed, esports has been referred to as the Wild West and – given that esports is an umbrella term for different games and stakeholders – esports "is ungovernable by one clear authority" (Scholz, 2019, p. 74). Given the power held by game publishers, there is little room in esports for the types of governing bodies found in sport. For some, this reflects the essence of esports (i.e., as a self-governed and bottom-up cultural phenomenon) but nonetheless it poses particular challenges for the implementation of industry-wide safeguarding standards. In sport, the management of safeguarding cases by a sport's respective national governing body is an important aspect of effective safeguarding practice (Rhind et al., 2015). In the absence of such governing bodies within esports, management of cases and dissemination of guidance becomes particularly difficult. Another area of concern relates to coaches

---

Box 12.2   Forms of harassment and abuse

Harassment and abuse can be expressed in five forms which may occur in combination or in isolation. These include:

1   Psychological abuse, which includes any unwelcome act including confinement, isolation, verbal assault, humiliation, intimidation, infantilisation, or any other treatment which may diminish the sense of identity, dignity, and self-worth.
2   Physical abuse, which includes any deliberate and unwelcome act – such as punching, beating, kicking, biting, and burning – that causes physical trauma or injury. Physical abuse can also include forcing an individual into excessive training or training while injured.
3   Sexual harassment, which includes any unwanted and unwelcome conduct of a sexual nature, whether verbal, non-verbal, or physical.
4   Sexual abuse, which includes any conduct of a sexual nature, whether non-contact, contact or penetrative, where consent is coerced/manipulated or is not or cannot be given.
5   Neglect, which refers to the failure to meet a child's basic needs or provide a minimum level of care to them, which is causing harm, allowing harm to be caused, or creating an imminent danger of harm.

It's also important to note that harassment and abuse can include a one-off incident or a series of incidents and occur either in person or online. Harassment may be deliberate, unsolicited, or coercive.

---

in esports, a role that does not currently require accreditation or certification, unlike in traditional sport. Indeed, there is currently no imperative for coaches to be regulated or have a background check. Nonetheless, coaches are in positions to gain access to young people in esports in both teams and private 1-1 settings. Esports therefore needs to urgently come to an alternative solution to avoid disjointed – or worse, competing – approaches to safeguarding that fail to protect children, vulnerable adults, and victims of abuse (Hatter, 2020).

Safeguarding involves several key elements. These include identifying potential risks and vulnerabilities, assessing the level of risk involved, developing strategies for prevention and intervention, providing support and assistance to those affected by abuse or neglect, and ensuring that appropriate action is taken when necessary. One essential aspect of safeguarding is communication. Effective communication between those working with vulnerable individuals can help identify potential risks early on and ensure that appropriate action is taken promptly. It also helps ensure that all parties involved are aware of their responsibilities in protecting vulnerable individuals. Another critical element of safeguarding is training. Professionals working with vulnerable individuals must receive adequate training on how to identify signs of abuse or neglect, how to respond appropriately if they suspect abuse or neglect has occurred, and how to work effectively with other professionals involved in the care of vulnerable individuals. These key elements appear within a framework of eight safeguards established by Rhind and Owusu-Sekyere (2018) as a result of their three-year research project into international perspectives on safeguarding. The below list provides an overview of these eight safeguards, and it's recommended that staff or practitioners working in esports check with their organisation if they are unsure on any of these points.

- Being aware of the organisational policies relevant to safeguarding and child protection
- Knowing who to go to within your organisation (e.g., Designated Safeguarding Lead) in order to report a concern
- Being able to locate sources of advice and support to help with safeguarding matters
- Taking proactive steps to minimise risks
- Being aware of any guidelines or codes of conduct that provide details of appropriate behaviour
- Utilising opportunities for training in the area of safeguarding
- Developing relationships with other people who can support you in your safeguarding role
- Regularly reviewing the organisation's safeguarding policy

12.1.2 Practical implications for esports to maintain player safety

Player safety in online gaming and esports environments is a crucial concern that has gained significant attention in recent years. With the rise of online gaming and esports, players are exposed to various risks such as cyberbullying, harassment, and physical injuries. Therefore, it is essential to ensure that players are safe while participating in these activities. Organisations can certainly play a key role here by emphasising the importance of safeguarding children to their members, ensuring members are aware of how safeguarding complements their strategy and overall vision, making policies readily available in which staff members' roles in relation to safeguarding are clearly explained, and finally encouraging coaches and other team staff to adopt pedagogies that promote health, welfare, and well-being (Rhind & Owusu-Sekyere, 2018). More general regulations and guidelines to ensure player safety are already evident for online gaming and esports platforms. These guidelines should include measures such as age restrictions, anti-bullying policies, privacy protection measures, and fair play rules. Additionally, game developers should design games with safety features such as parental controls that limit access to inappropriate content. Of course, all of these efforts must be implemented alongside education. Players should be educated on how to identify potential risks and how to report any incidents of harassment or bullying. Furthermore, parents should also be educated on how to monitor their children's online activities and protect them from potential dangers. Indeed, parental awareness of their child's online activity and experiences more generally is low (Livingstone et al., 2011).

In sport, it is commonplace for safeguarding checks such as Disclosure and Barring Service (DBS) checks to be required when applying for certain roles or voluntary positions that involve working with children or vulnerable adults. While these checks can help to flag potential concerns and perhaps deter perpetrators, it's important to emphasise that background checks represent one part of the broader safeguarding system that is necessary to prevent abuse. Safeguarding cases may also occur between individuals that do not require a background check, such as a player's peers (Alexander et al., 2011). For an esports organisation that is recruiting for a team staff role or volunteer, it's recommended that the recruitment process includes interviews and professional references to supplement background checks (Hedges, 2015). While this is not yet mandatory within esports, rigorous recruitment and vetting procedures such as these are a step towards preventing safeguarding cases occurring and are thus in everyone's interest.

As mentioned previously, another challenge in esports is that many coaches practise on a self-employed basis by offering private coaching within a specific game (Hatter, 2020). As such, the International Federation of Esports Coaches (IFoEC) – a global organisation dedicated to the professional development of coaches in esports – established an online membership directory in 2020 to showcase coaches that had signed-up with a background check. IFoEC also released a whitepaper on safeguarding in esports (Hatter, 2020) and a guidance document for esports organisations as to their safeguarding obligations (Hatter, 2021). The guidance document sets out a number of steps to raise safeguarding standards within esports, such as the creation of a safeguarding board to bring together expertise from both esports and safeguarding, appointing a safeguarding commissioner to have oversight of policy and implementation, and establishing a code of conduct.

One final point to keep in mind is that everyone has a duty to share in the safeguarding and the welfare of vulnerable groups regardless of their role or responsibility. Esports can provide a means to inspire and encourage vulnerable individuals, but through its various digital platforms, and lack of both awareness and regulation, it can also give those involved a position of influence and an opportunity to do harm – intentionally or not. Only through an ongoing, coherent, and collective approach to safeguarding can we minimise the risks to children and vulnerable individuals.

12.1.3 Safeguarding – Conclusion

We have outlined above some of the key concepts and practices within safeguarding, and described some of the challenges and recommended practices to safeguarding in esports. It's important to highlight, however, that any preventative measures put in place to prevent abuse will not be 100% effective. The aim should always be to reduce the risk, respond to threats as they change, and to innovate. Given the aforementioned issues around governance in esports, ultimately the industry needs to work together to establish a coherent and ongoing approach to safeguarding.

In conclusion, safeguarding plays a vital role in protecting vulnerable individuals from harm or abuse. By identifying potential risks early on and taking appropriate action when necessary, we can help ensure that everyone receives the care they deserve while maintaining their dignity and respect as human beings.

12.2 Cheating in esports

Cheating in esports has been a growing concern in recent years. With the rise of competitive gaming, e'athletes are constantly looking for ways to gain an advantage over their opponents. Cheating can take many forms, for example cheat tools (software) such as aimbots (to improve a player's aim) and wallhacks (allowing a player to see through walls) to exploiting glitches and bugs in the game. Other examples include stream sniping, in which a player sees the location of opponents by watching their live stream. Cheating in esports is also possible through the use of hardware although it is arguably less common, for example, programming a mouse to perform certain movements that would be impossible without it.

One of the biggest cheating scandals in professional esports occurred in 2014. Several high-profile players, including Hovik "KQLY" Tovmassian, were caught using a cheat program by Valve's anti-cheat-software. The players – and their teams – were subsequently banned from competing in the upcoming CS:GO Major Championship at Dreamhack Winter, set to start nine days later and which had a $250,000 prize pool. This scandal was damaging on numerous levels, not least due to the lingering uncertainty about the extent of the cheating. For example, there were doubts about whether KQLY cheated at a LAN tournaments or purely in online practice environments.

Other notable examples of cheating include the "Olofboost", in which Fnatic CS:GO player olofmeister used his teammates to jump and then balance on a pixel that commanded significant map vision. From this position, olofmeister was able to pick off opponents and lead his team to a victory in the quarterfinals of the 2014 Dreamhack Winter Major. Dubbed the olofboost, this was an example of "pixel walking", which is banned in official matches. Another notable scandal occurred in 2019 when a professional Overwatch player named Ellie was revealed to be a fake persona and actually was an established player Punisher. This caused controversy and raised questions about gender discrimination within esports.

Cheating scandals not only damage the reputation of individual players but also tarnish the integrity of the entire industry. The consequences of cheating in esports can be severe. In some cases, cheating can result in disqualification or even legal action. To combat cheating in esports, many organisations have implemented strict rules and regulations. Anti-cheat software is also commonly used to detect and prevent cheating during gameplay. However, these measures are not foolproof, and some players still manage to cheat undetected. Ultimately, it is up to individual players to uphold the values of fair play and sportsmanship in esports. Cheating may provide temporary benefits, but it ultimately undermines the integrity of competitive gaming as a whole.

12.3 Gambling

Gambling in esports often falls under the following forms:

1 Skin betting: This involves using in-game items or virtual currency, such as "skins," as a form of currency to place bets on esports matches. Skins are virtual items that can be earned or purchased in-game and have real-world value on trading platforms.
2 Traditional betting: This involves placing bets on the outcome of esports matches using traditional forms of currency, such as cash or credit.
3 Fantasy esports: This involves creating a virtual team of esports players and competing against other players based on the actual performance of the players in real-world esports matches.

Gambling in esports has become increasingly popular in recent years. The revenue generated by gambling in professional esports is difficult to estimate accurately, as the industry is relatively new and rapidly evolving. Estimates have placed esports annual gambling revenue between $1.5B USD and $7.4B USD prior to 2020 (Grove, 2016; Warman, 2017). In 2022, it was revealed that the global esports betting market has an estimated worth of $10B USD as of 2021, and is expected to reach $24B USD by 2028 (Absolute Reports, 2022). Despite the growth of betting interest in esports likely being a side-effect of the rapid growth of esports itself, gambling in esports also poses significant risks. These include the potential for match-fixing and the exploitation of underage players. Many countries have implemented regulations to address these issues, including age restrictions and licensing requirements for gambling operators. Esports organisations and event organisers have also implemented strict rules and policies to prevent and detect gambling-related misconduct.

There have been several instances of illegal betting in professional esports. One notable example is the "Operation Power Play" investigation conducted by Australian police in 2019. The investigation revealed a widespread illegal betting ring involving professional CS:GO matches. The betting ring was reportedly run by a criminal syndicate based in Australia and involved over 20 professional esports players from Australia and the United States. Another example is the "Skincoin" scandal that occurred in 2018. The scandal involved a Russian betting website that used the cryptocurrency Skincoin to facilitate illegal gambling on various esports events, including CS:GO and Dota 2 matches. The website reportedly operated without a license and allowed users to place bets using virtual items, including skins and other in-game items. In both cases, the individuals involved were charged with illegal gambling and faced significant fines and potential prison time. These cases highlight the need for increased regulation and oversight in the esports betting industry to prevent illegal activities and protect the integrity of professional esports competitions.

It's important to note that gambling in esports also includes traditional forms of betting, such as sportsbooks and online gambling sites, which have been offering esports betting markets in recent years. Additionally, the growing popularity of fantasy esports and other innovative forms of esports betting are also contributing to the growth of the industry. Although gambling and betting will be part and parcel of the esports industry, education of players and spectators and prevention of criminal practices needs to be addressed.

References

Absolute Reports. (April, 2022). *2021–203 Report on global esports betting market by player, region, type, application and sales channel.* Retrieved from https://www.absolutereports.com/2021-2030-report-on-global-esports-betting-market-20729767

Alexander, K., Stafford, A., & Lewis, R. (2011). *The experiences of children participating in organised sport in the UK.* London: NSPCC.

Grove, C. (2016). *Esports and gambling: Where's the action?* Eilers & Krejcik Gaming. Retrieved from https://www.thelines.com/wp-content/uploads/2018/03/Esports-and-Gambling.pdf Hatter, M. (2020). *The challenge of safeguarding in esports white paper.* Retrieved from https://markhatterassociates.org/pages/whitepapers

Hatter, M. (2021). *Keeping children and young people safe in esports - Guidance for esports and gaming organisations.* Retrieved from https://www.ifoec.com/safeguarding

Hedges, A. (2015). Safeguarding in sport. *Sport in Society, 18*(5), 614–625. https://doi.org/10.1080/17430437.2014.976010

Livingstone, S., Haddon, L. G., Görzig, A., & Ólafsson, K. (2011). *Risks and Safety on the Internet: The perspective of European Children - Full findings and policy implications from the EU Kids Online survey of 9-16 year olds and their parents in 25 countries.* London: London School of Economics and Political Science.

Rhind, D., McDermott, J., Lambert, E., & Koleva, I. (2015). A review of safeguarding cases in sport. *Child Abuse Review, 24*(6), 418–426.

Rhind, D., & Owusu-Sekyere, F. (2018). *International safeguards for children in sport: Developing and embedding a safeguarding culture.* New York: Routledge.

Scholz, T. M. (2019). *ESports is business. Management in the world of competitive gaming.* Cham, Switzerland: Palgrave Macmillan.

Warman, P. (2017). *Esports revenues will reach $696 million this year and grow to $1.5 billion by 2020 as brand investment doubles.* Newzoo. Retrieved from https://newzoo.com/insights/articles/esports-revenues-will-reach-696-million-in-2017/

13 Key considerations for the future

Craig McNulty

We are in an exciting new era of esports, with seemingly boundless opportunities for players, practitioners, and researchers. The uptake of esports as a potential career path is rapidly growing, with interest being fostered at a grassroots level. The increase in professional and amateur player-base has attracted coaches, performance and health practitioners, sponsorship, the formation of new and exciting leagues, and an abundance of research opportunities to support e'athletes and continue the positive advancement of the industry. This book has covered a range of topics within esports, from coaching and the environment of esports, to physiological and nutritional health and performance, to psychology and esports technology. Within its chapters researcher and practitioner' knowledge has helped define our understanding of some of the key topic areas of interest for e'athletes and coaches, from grassroots to the world stage. We are still at an early stage of understanding the global phenomenon of esports; however, we hope this book has given some valuable insights into the depth of the esports industry, environment, and e'athlete's performance and health.

The following outlines some of the key considerations across the previous 12 chapters. These points are those that the authors believe either to be informative or to have the potential for immediate practical application:

- Esports has rapidly evolved in recent years, with a growing player-base, increased spectators, broadcasting opportunities, and revenue. While there are many similarities between esports and traditional sports, there are also key differences that need to be addressed to ensure the health and performance of e'athletes. To achieve this, research is needed to identify the determinants of performance and best practices for training and competition structures. This requires a needs analysis of game titles and players in relation to psychophysiological research to inform exercise programming. Assessments of strength, cardiovascular fitness, cognition, and body composition can also inform nutritional planning and interventions.
- It is important to provide psychological support to e'athletes, especially at the elite level, to manage stress, develop coping strategies, and enhance performance and psychological well-being. The motivational orientation of e'athletes is also critical for talent development, engagement, and performance, so it is

DOI: 10.4324/9781003322382-13

essential to develop a growth mindset and intrinsic motivation through the development of psychological skills training programs.

- Team cohesion is important for success in esports, but there is still much research to be done to develop evidence-based strategies that can enhance task and social cohesion. Effective communication during training and competition is also critical to promote team interaction, cohesion, and performance while reducing misunderstandings.
- Toxicity in esports is a major issue that must be addressed by e'athletes and the industry as a whole. Esports training and performance take place online and in-person at LAN tournaments or on-stage games, so it is important to be aware of the challenges and demands of players and coaches in these different settings. Preparing for in-person tournaments requires effective planning, training in simulated conditions, familiarising players with the venue conditions, and developing routines.
- Coaches play a critical role in esports, but research on this role is still scarce. It is recommended that coaches consider nested planning, aligning overall goals with month-to-month and day-to-day team activities. Safeguarding is also essential in esports, particularly for children and other vulnerable individuals. Measures need to be taken to protect them from harm, abuse, or neglect.
- This book also highlights the importance of talent identification and development pathways, coaching education, and measures to prevent overuse injuries and obesity. Lastly, maintaining the integrity of the industry and specific games within it is crucial through addressing instances of cheating and gambling in esports.

Of course, these are just some key takeaways. Esports as an industry has claimed its position as one of the biggest competitive phenomena on Earth; however, esports research is still in its infancy. We, as a collective of esports practitioners, e'athletes, researchers, developers, and competition organisers, continue to push the boundaries to allow continued growth of esports. With this growth, we will discover new knowledge and practice, as well as determine where our limits in understanding lay. As a community we should push for best evidence-based practice across all layers of esports.

We are truly excited to be part of the journey of esports.

Craig, Remco, Matt & Kabir.

Index

Note: **Bold** page numbers refer to tables and *italic* page numbers refer to figures.

For Product Safety Concerns and Information please contact our EU
representative GPSR@taylorandfrancis.com Taylor & Francis Verlag GmbH,
Kaufingerstraße 24, 80331 München, Germany

Printed and bound by CPI Group (UK) Ltd, Croydon, CR0 4YY
08/06/2025
01897004-0002